GHOSTS
of Gettysburg
VIII

Spirits, Apparitions and Haunted Places of the Battlefield

by
Mark Nesbitt

Second Chance Publications
Gettysburg, PA 17325

Copyright 2018 Mark Nesbitt
Published by Second Chance Publications
P.O. Box 3126
Gettysburg, PA. 17325

WARNING! The stories herein are fully protected by U. S. Federal copyright laws. Unauthorized copying, reproduction, recording, broadcasting, derivative works and public performance, by any individual or company without written consent of the publisher and author are strictly prohibited. Federal copyright laws will be vigorously enforced and infringements will be prosecuted to the fullest extent of the law, which can include damages and lawyers' fees to be paid by the infringer of copyright.

ISBN: 0-9995795-2-5
ISBN-13: 978-0-9995795-2-7

Photos by Mark and Carol Nesbitt unless otherwise credited.
Original cover design by Ryan C. Stouch

**To Maddy
From Pop-Pop**

TABLE OF CONTENTS

Introduction 1

A Haunted *Ghosts of Gettysburg* Book 5

From Humble Clay Great Captains Rise 7

Reading, Writing & Wraiths at the High Street School 13

Strange Visitors at the Inn 21

Through a Glass, Darkly 31

The Ghosts of Springs Avenue 49

Again, the Devil's Den 59

The Triangular Field 71

Little Round Top 81

Déjà Vu 93
    The Texan 96
    The Recurring Sightings of General Reynolds 99
    The House on Carlisle Street 111
    The Blue Boy, the Typewriter Lady, & the Party Ghost 120

Beings of Light 127

Sources 137

Acknowledgments 139

About the Author 140

There is a fatality, a feeling so irresistible and inevitable that it has the force of doom, which almost invariably compels human beings to linger around and haunt, ghostlike, the spot where some great and marked event has given color to their lifetime....

—Nathaniel Hawthorne, *The Scarlet Letter*

INTRODUCTION

What is essential is invisible to the eye.
—Antoine de Saint-Exupéry,
The Little Prince.

One of the reasons it has taken so long to write *Ghosts of Gettysburg VIII* is that I have been working on various other writing projects. Since *Ghosts of Gettysburg VII* came out in 2011, I wrote, co-wrote, re-wrote and published six other books: *Civil War Ghost Trails* (2012); *Blood & Ghosts* (2012); *If the South Won Gettysburg, 150th Anniversary Edition* (2013); *Haunted Crime Scenes* (2014); *Cursed in Pennsylvania* (2016); and *Cursed in Virginia* (2017).

All were exciting projects. But still in the back of my mind were all the stories sent to me and told to me by individuals who had experienced the unexplainable on and around the Gettysburg Battlefield

Hundreds of stories were never used because of the books' site-specific format. In other words, I was limited to geographical places on the battlefield (like Devil's Den, Little Round Top, or the field of Picket's Charge) that yielded the most stories. I set aside places with just one or two stories.

I decided to take a different approach with this book. I am not going to limit myself to sites that have the most stories associated with them. We're going to go outside the normal "boundaries" of the battle based on how the stories fit into the reasons ghosts are created, why they seem to linger (or are trapped) at one place, how these accounts fit into the way spirits manifest themselves, and why they want to remind us of their existence.

That ghosts exist cannot be doubted any more. Thousands of accounts have been collected and witnessed by myself and others at just Civil War battlefields alone, not to mention battlefields of other wars and various sites around the world from all of history.

Why they exist is also, seemingly, common knowledge: Their mortality was cut short too soon; their lives were snuffed out violently; they were slain so suddenly they don't realize they're dead; they left unfinished business behind; they were too young to die; they were in extreme emotional stress when their lives were extinguished, leaving behind the imprint of their existence in vague, dim, shadowy forms.

But now I am interested in *how* they continue to manifest themselves, and the questions maddeningly outnumber the answers: How do they (or better yet, *we*) continue to exist after earthly death? Where do ghosts dwell? Another dimension? A parallel universe, yet invisible? How do they gather the energy needed to become visible, or make noise, or move physical objects before our eyes and ears? Do they want to communicate with us, as it appears they do? What priceless knowledge must they have to impart? How can we facilitate and amplify this communication?

Along with more ghost stories about Gettysburg, you will read stories about places with a Gettysburg connection. You will also read about ghostly manifestations that have re-occurred in Gettysburg, sometimes decades later to different people at a different time, a sort of ghostly *déjà vu*. These are more than interesting; they represent serious, evidently replicable, data. There will also be connections made between the ghosts of Gettysburg and solid scientific theories from famous psychologists to ground breaking physicists. This is something I've wanted to do for years: to lend some legitimacy to the data on the paranormal I've gathered over the decades. There will be some proven science for you to ponder and place where you'd like in your understanding of ghosts.

Which leads me to another point: I'm tired of ghost books and tours and television programs that seem only to want to prove that ghosts exist. It's been done. After collecting some *thirteen hundred* stories from all the major Civil War sites around the country (see *Civil War Ghost Trails*), I certainly do not need any more convincing that ghosts exist.

Another thing I've concluded after decades of studying war, and the American Civil War in particular: Gettysburg—and other battlefields—are huge *laboratories* for the study of paranormal anomalies we identify as ghosts. Because of the violence, the suddenness, the youthful deaths and the explosion of emotion associated with human travail in combat, battles provide the "perfect storm" for creating ghosts *en masse*. The battlefields upon which humans were slain in large numbers seem to be the dwelling-place for soldiers' souls.

I am lucky because Gettysburg has been a part of my life for nearly sixty years. Between youthful visits, my time working as a park ranger living on the battlefield, my living within sight of the first day's battlefield for fifteen years, and owning a business which compels me to return to Gettysburg almost weekly, I have had unique access to one of—if not *the*—most haunted site, acre for acre, in America.

How many ages hence
Shall this our lofty scene be acted over,
In states unborn and accents yet unknown!

—William Shakespeare, *Julius Caesar*

A HAUNTED *GHOSTS OF GETTYSBURG* BOOK

The most beautiful thing we can experience is the mysterious.
It is the source of all true art and science.

—Albert Einstein

Writing classes teach students to write effectively, meaning be concise, precise, always writing to the point you are trying to make.

I have always tried to write "affectively," meaning that writing should move people into some sort of action.

I received a letter from a woman who sent me a story about her paranormal experience years before, which I included in *Ghosts of Gettysburg V*. She had read all my other books and was in the process of reading the fifth volume. She said that the book was taking her a while to finish, not because it was boring, but because it was "draining." She compared it to the story of a house cleansing I wrote about in my second book, how emotionally exhausting it was for the priest involved.

She said she had finally finished the book and dozed off for a few minutes. She was awakened by her newborn daughter crying and she realized that her house was icy-cold, "bone-chilling," to use her words. It was in the 70s outside, but inside she was "freezing not just cold, but cold to the bone." The coldness lasted for about an hour. "Then my house was toasty warm again and my daughter stopped fussing." She thought it was unusual that it happened right after finishing my book and wondered if anyone else had a similar experience.

Talk about "affective" writing.

But in the back of my mind, with what I know about ghosts after chasing them in Gettysburg for over half my life, the phenomena may not have been completely attributed to my writing skills. It just may have had a supernatural cause.

People have been "affected" by things they have brought home from Gettysburg: rocks, pieces of wood, souvenirs, and now apparently books.

And, no doubt, they have been "affected" by lasting memories of the place, haunting them into some action, so to speak, for years after their first visit.

Much like how the soldiers were "affected" after *their* first visit to Gettysburg.

The place grows on you. It may even grow *in* you.

I came to Gettysburg during my childhood and teen years in the role of a tourist; then as a park ranger right after college. After that, I stayed to write. For nearly thirty years.

I heard years later that a high school girlfriend once warned someone who said they were going to visit Gettysburg not to go: "You'll never leave. The place swallows you up and you're never heard from again."

Perhaps.

Perhaps.

FROM HUMBLE CLAY GREAT CAPTAINS RISE

...in the absence of a home I wish I could purchase Stratford. That is the only place I could go to, now accessible to us, that would inspire me with feelings of pleasure and local love.... I wonder if it is for sale and how much.

—Gen. Robert E. Lee to his wife, December 25, 1861

One of the names linked imperishably with Gettysburg is, of course, General Robert E. Lee.

He was born into one of America's most prominent families who settled in the Northern Neck of Virginia, between the Potomac and Rappahannock Rivers. In 1641, the Lees began to build an empire based upon land ownership. Planters, merchants, ship owners, Lees also served in the General Assembly, the colonial government of Virginia.

Robert E. Lee's father, Henry Lee, III, married a nineteen-year-old second cousin Matilda Lee. They settled in her family's magnificent plantation mansion "Stratford Hall," overlooking the Potomac River.

Matilda died in 1790. In 1793, Henry married Ann Hill Carter, from another esteemed Virginia family. They resided at Stratford Hall.

In 1806, after bearing four children Ann discovered she was again pregnant. On January 19, 1807, at Stratford Hall, she gave birth to another son, whom she named after her brothers, Robert and Edward.

Due to the difficulties and expenses of running such a large mansion, when Robert was four years old, his family moved from spacious Stratford Hall to a small, two-story house in Alexandria, Virginia. While Robert's childhood at Stratford was short, his emotional connection with the place would last a lifetime.

Stratford Hall

As he grew to manhood, Lee's life, in spite of his famous name, was anything but easy. He attended the United States Military Academy at West Point and graduated as an engineer.

He married well, to Mary Custis and into the family of his boyhood hero George Washington, and fathered seven children. But his advancement as a career soldier was agonizingly slow and consisted of long stretches away from his family, dull engineering work on numerous forts around the country, and a short but distinguished combat career in the Mexican War. After thirty-two years in the army, he was still a colonel.

When the Civil War broke out in 1861, Lee had an agonizing choice to make. He was offered a major-generalship and a command in the United States army. Being an army officer, he realized that secession of the states from the Union could be considered rebellion and an officer going to that side could be considered a traitor. But when President Abraham Lincoln called for troops to put down the rebellion and Virginia finally voted for secession, Lee realized that he would be called on to invade his home state and perhaps fight and kill fellow Virginians. His choice was clear: He resigned his commission in the U.S. Army.

He eventually became the most famous of all Confederate generals, leading its largest army, winning numerous battles until the Confederate catastrophe at Gettysburg, holding on tenaciously until finally forced to surrender at Appomattox Court House. Though his name is linked forever with the Confederate Army, his command of it lasted two months short of three years.

On July 16, 2010, in preparation for a "Mysterious Journey's Weekend" event, Laine, our medium, Carol, my wife, and I did a preliminary paranormal investigation of the famed Stratford Hall.

Once a vast plantation, Stratford Hall is now a well managed historic site with restored buildings, gardens, tours of the great house, modern buildings for meetings, conferences and weddings, a research library, and accommodations for overnight visitors including a dining hall and lodging.

As part of our preliminary investigations, I interviewed staff members for any paranormal events they witnessed or ghost stories they may have heard. Like most historic sites, Stratford Hall has its share.

One guide at Stratford said that a housekeeper was sent to clean the library. She came back a few minutes later saying she didn't want to disturb the man who was there. He was sitting at a desk going over some papers and looked distressed. She and her supervisor went to the library, but, to her surprise, there was no one there. Remembering the history of Stratford, they recalled that the famed "Light Horse

Harry" Lee, more the soldier and politician than the businessman, met virtual financial ruin at Stratford and ended up in debtor's prison. Could the specter they saw in the library be Robert E. Lee's father still tormented by his debts?

Then there was the night watchman who heard a knock at the door late one evening. He opened it to see a little boy dressed in purple pants. Apparently mute, he motioned for the watchman to follow, which he did until the boy passed *through* a fence without the aid of the gate. The watchman insisted he hadn't been scared of the apparition; he just "decided" to return his office.

One woman who guided at Stratford continually saw those light anomalies called orbs often coming right at her. She also felt insistent tugging on her period day dress, as if some unseen child wanted her attention.

Martha, a long time guide, also saw a twelve or thirteen-year-old boy standing in the doorway to the kitchen outbuilding while she gave her tour. When she dismissed her group, she went to look for the boy since she knew there were no school groups at Stratford that day. In spite of all the open ground around and an exhaustive search, she found no trace of the boy.

She also related the story of a little girl on one of her tours who became very upset. When asked what the problem was, she said she had seen a little girl sitting at the window when they toured the nursery. She said she looked so sad. As the tour was leaving, she went back to see the little girl but she had vanished.

Melody, another guide at the interview, mistakenly thought Martha was referring to the story about a little girl who started crying on a tour, but the circumstances were different. They were touring the mother's bedchambers, not the nursery. The young tourist also saw a little girl, but what upset her most is that she was "hovering" above the floor in the bedchambers.

Melody recounted one more story about a child ghost. One of the guides was locking up for the night, coming down the servant's stairway. When he turned around he saw a lady in a gray cape bending down next to a child. He lost sight of them for just a second as he went back to tell them that the place was closed. When he rounded the corner, they had disappeared.

History tells us that one of the tragedies of Stratford Hall was that a two year old girl, Margaret Lee, fell down the great stone staircase of Stratford Hall and was killed. Whenever the ghost of a little girl appears, she is remembered.

While I collected several good ghost stories from the staff at Stratford Hall that day, little did I know that I was to be a victim of one of the ghosts at Lee's birthplace.

In addition to the lodgings for the general public, there are also private log cottages owned by members of the board of directors. With just the three of us visiting, the management put us up in one of the cottages. There was a central great room with separate bedrooms and baths on either side.

After our planning meetings with the staff and dinner, the three of us returned to the cottage and went to our respective bedrooms.

Sometime in the middle of the night, around 2 A.M., I woke up thinking Carol had gotten up and was standing beside her side of the bed. I asked, "Are you alright?" and she answered, "Yeah, I'm fine." Her voice, however, came from the bed right next to me, not the side of the bed where I saw the figure.

I started to look at the figure—I should say "mass"—next to Carol's side of the bed. It was then that I noticed that it was far too large to be Carol; it took up one-third of the side of the bed as it stood there. It seemed to be "dressed" in a flowing, dark, thick, robe-type garment with numerous folds and a hood. I got a distinct impression of a dark green hue to the mass. I watched it for nearly a minute trying to figure out what it was, and finally decided that it must be the dark area on the wall between the windows in the bedroom. I figured I'd verify my theory the next morning, rolled over to face the other wall and suddenly got a distinct chill running up my spine to the nape of my neck. I shook it off and convinced myself it was my imagination.

The next morning, the first thing I did was to check the wall where I saw the dark mass. I was surprised to see that there was only one window in that wall and it was in the center where I saw the dark mass. This eliminated my theory that it was the wall between two windows that I had seen. Obviously, there had been something blocking out any light coming from the central window in the wall.

When we saw Laine that morning, I casually mentioned it to her. She knows that, in spite of the fact that I have been in the paranormal business for decades, I rarely have paranormal experiences and even more rarely, visuals. She got a rather sheepish look and a half smile grew on her face. Carol and I looked at her. "Oops," she said.

"What did you do?" Carol said as if speaking to a naughty child.

Laine related how she was being bugged by the spirit of a Civil War soldier in her room from the time she retired until about 2 A.M. She finally told him to leave so she could get some sleep. He asked her where he should go. She replied "Go to Mark's room. He can't see you."

Apparently he did.

Apparently, frighteningly, I could.

READING, WRITING & WRAITHS AT THE HIGH STREET SCHOOL

You may relish him more in the soldier than in the scholar.
—William Shakespeare, *Othello*

Along the *Ghosts of Gettysburg Candlelight Walking Tours* Baltimore Street route are two sites that are almost at opposite ends of the tour, but are closely connected.

Guides take customers south on Baltimore Street to "Alumni Park," dedicated to graduates of the local Gettysburg Area School District. There the guides tell customers the harrowing tales of the Rupp Tannery Civil War era house across Lefever Street, of the two women who once ran an art gallery and how one had accused the other of rearranging her miniature soldier display time after time. The other denied touching it. The mystery was solved when the first woman saw a figure dressed like a Union officer complete with high boots, saber, frock coat and gauntlets slowly enter through a sealed-off door. He stood for a few seconds, looked at her and vanished before her astonished eyes. After that, she assumed it was the ghostly officer who was unimpressed with her tactical arrangement of the tiny soldiers and continually rearranged them to reflect his memories of the battle.

The mystery deepened, however, when the other woman, after hearing the description of the soldier said, "No, that's not what the soldier I saw looked like," and described a tall, gaunt, red-headed soldier in a "pink" uniform with a long rifle. She couldn't have known that some Confederates at Gettysburg wore "butternut" dyed uniforms, which in the right light, could take on a pinkish hue.

Rupp Tannery now Mr. G's Ice Cream Shop

According to two of our *Ghosts of Gettysburg Candlelight Walking Tours* guides and fifty or more customers, a number of soldiers gathered one night to roam around inside the Rupp Tannery office for at least forty-five minutes, long after the business that occupied the building had closed for the day. They could be seen leaning against the mantle, peeping out the windows, and even sitting at a phantom table eating a phantom meal.

East High Street, for such a short stretch, has more ghost stories per linear yard than any other street in Gettysburg. Perhaps it's because it was once the location of two cemeteries—one across the street from the Old German Reformed Church on the corner of East High Street and Stratton Street (the church that, while serving as a hospital surgical orderlies had to drill holes in the floor to let the blood drain)—and the other just behind the Presbyterian Church (now the parking lot) which faces Baltimore street.

The cemeteries were eventually closed and the bodies "removed" to other places of burial.

To guarantee that 100 percent of the bodies were removed from the cemeteries on East High Street would be foolhardy. Some, no doubt, endured the rumbling of heavy machinery as parking lots were built, then maintained for the succession of organizations which have occupied the old jail building (currently the Borough Building) and the Presbyterian Church. Rest in Peace in the East High Street Cemeteries? Doubtful, at best.

But for students of early Gettysburg, their classrooms were in the private homes of teachers for some twenty-three years. In 1857, the large brick Common Schoolhouse was built on East High Street and the students were consolidated there. According to 1860 records, each teacher had 70 pupils on their rolls. For a century the Common School Building served the young scholars of the Gettysburg community well.

If, as many expert paranormalists theorize, energy plays a large part in a haunting, schools must have at least residual hauntings associated with them. Of course, Gettysburg schools have the added energy of the supernatural: nearly every one was built on some part of the battlefield where men's energies were at their peak struggling for their lives and often losing that struggle on the very spot where someday some young Gettysburg student might study or dance or play sports.

The evidence that in Gettysburg you just never know when you're going to hear a ghost story or two comes from an incident on August 4, 2017. While standing in the middle of the street, I heard one from a gentleman working on the road next to the *Ghosts of Gettysburg* tour headquarters.

They had just finished blacktopping Breckenridge Street at the end of July 2017. I noticed that some of the blacktop had partially clogged the drain in the curb for our sump pump. I saw some of the workers doing the blacktopping and went out to ask them about it. They were as cordial as could be as they used a blowtorch on the clump and pulled the clog out. The one gentleman was joking with me. "Now will you tell us a ghost story? I know who you are. I have a couple of your books."

I begged off on the ghost story as I was helping Katie, my daughter and manager of the business, open up. When I came out with my granddaughter Maddy, the workers were still there and the one who recognized me said, "I've got a ghost story for *you!*"

They worked for a company that does a lot of the repaving and road repair on the National Park. Nearly all of the work is done overnight, after the park is closed, so as not to disturb visitation. He said it was about 5:30 A.M., still dark before dawn, when he was walking near the Wheatfield to get to the paving machine.

"I was walking along and from behind me I heard, from a distance no farther than I am from you right now," he gestured across the three feet between us, "a horse whinny. I spun around and there was nothing behind me."

I mentioned that I have a number of stories involving people hearing horses—whinnying, clopping their hooves at a walk, trot or gallop—from visitors to town and the park.

He said, "And that's not all. My wife worked at the old Keefauver School and had a really strange experience."

Keefauver was one of the Gettysburg elementary schools built after the Common School was no longer useful for classrooms. It was eventually torn down to make room for the enlarged junior high school. The most disturbing thing about it was that it had been built just to the north of Culp's Hill and within sight of the famous (and haunted) Culp Farm.

He said his wife was working late into the night at the school. It was dark, but a co-worker and she looked up to see a man standing in the doorway. They knew it couldn't have been a prowler because, according to her husband, "It was only half a man, from the waist up." It lingered momentarily, as if wondering what these people were doing in his space, then, as if realizing that he was actually in *their* space, vanished before their eyes.

A former student? An old administrator or teacher? A soldier who left this earth on that spot where the door to the modern classroom was built? Imponderables, one and all.

But the old Common School building certainly has its own strange happenings, and may be the place where spirits consent to being photographed.

Common School now the Adams County Housing Authority

During the first day of the battle, July 1, 1863, wounded Union soldiers began trickling back from the aid stations just behind the battle lines to the west, north and east of the town of Gettysburg. Surgeons had commandeered most of the large public buildings—the Adams County Courthouse, "Old Dorm" on the Pennsylvania College campus, and most of the churches—for what they knew was sure to come: scores of injured men seeking help. Their estimate of the numbers of men to be hurt and maimed was horrifyingly low.

The Common School became a Union hospital…first. After the Confederates were victorious on the first day and drove the Union troops through the town and past East High Street, the

Common School building then became a hospital for Confederates as well. Later, when the Confederates pulled their lines back and relinquished the town prior to their retreat, the Common School became a Union hospital again—but also housing wounded Confederates.

Though the co-mingled wounded were too sick and weak to fight each other, they were still segregated by floors—northerners on the first floor and southerners above them. A chaplain, on August 7, 1863, wrote that there were still about forty Union and thirty Confederate soldiers left in the building out of some 230 that he had counted before.

While the battle raged, one infantryman from the 17th Connecticut who was a patient in the Common School hospital recalled bullets and shell fragments "rattling" against the sturdy walls of the school. Another Union soldier, when Confederates captured and occupied the town, hid in the belfry for four days with just a few drops of water in his canteen and a couple of hardtack crackers.

Bell in Alumni Park

The belfry no longer exists. The bell he hid beside is the one now displayed in Alumni Park.

*Ghost caught in right window of ACHA Building.
Photo courtesy of Cathy Passiatore*

Today the Adams County Housing Authority occupies the old school building. But even our guides, who should be jaded to these events by now, are surprised at the large number of photos of the building taken by our customers showing strange images. In fact, they always encourage our tours to take extra photos because it is so supernaturally photogenic.

A warning. Not every "face" seemingly peering out from the windows of the old school building is a ghost. Trees and lights, sometimes unnoticed *behind* the photographer, will reflect in the window panes, then the psychological phenomenon of pareidolia—the tendency for the human brain to "connect the dots" of a visual image, or recognize something familiar in a matrix—will take over. A good paranormal researcher will inspect all the elements and conditions surrounding the taking of a photograph, as well as taking several photographs of the same subject or area. Reflected images will usually change in each exposure, eliminating the perceived "ghostly image."

The ghosts of Gettysburg may be abundant...but they are also elusive.

STRANGE VISITORS AT THE INN

I have supp'd full with horrors;
Direness, familiar to my slaughterous thoughts,
Cannot once start me.

—William Shakespeare, *Macbeth*

There is an inn not too far from the town of Gettysburg that I have been familiar with since the 1970s. When I was a park ranger and it was a private home owned by another ranger, I stopped there, admired his lovely garden and drank a beer or two with him.

Baladerry Inn

Back then it was a small two-story brick building typical of the type built prior to when the American Civil War brought its terror, horror and slaughter on a Biblical scale to the fields and farms around peaceful Gettysburg. Some of the bricks used in its construction were probably molded and fired locally, since few of the settlers on the outskirts of town could afford the harder, high quality, red brick from Philadelphia.

Gregory A. Coco's book, *A Vast Sea of Misery*, a compendium of the hospitals after the battle, does not list the house as a field hospital. But it is close to a road, which is dotted with the U.S. Government Field Hospital markers for the various army corps engaged in the battle. In that vicinity, where many of the wounded were brought right after the battle, it is more likely that it just wasn't officially listed as a hospital. Yet, in some way, the house, barn, or fields, were no doubt occupied by the bloody and battered human remnants of the vicious fighting and witnessed the passing to another plane the mortal souls of many.

Later, when I was a freelance writer and researcher living in Gettysburg, I was again invited to the house by the new owner. The garden was gone and an entire wing had been added to the former farmhouse, built mostly over the garden site. Tennis courts were also added. Later, the house was turned into a bed and breakfast, which it has been ever since, although with several different owners and names.

Often people who rent out rooms at local B & Bs will request rooms in the more recently built sections of the inns, reasoning that the newer sections would not be haunted and so they would provide a peaceful night's sleep. What they forget is that the newer additions may have been built over gravesites from the battle, or even from previous early settlers of the land.

What most people don't realize about the dead after the Battle of Gettysburg was that every deceased soldier was buried at least twice—once where he fell on the battlefield, and once when his body was exhumed and taken to his permanent burial site. In the case of most of the Union soldiers, they were taken to the newly purchased (in 1863) land on Cemetery Hill, adjacent to Evergreen Cemetery, the cemetery for Gettysburg citizens. The new cemetery would be called the Soldiers' National Cemetery and be dedicated and consecrated on November 19, 1863, by President Abraham Lincoln. Burials would continue for months after he delivered his famous Gettysburg Address, but the soldiers would now lie in consecrated ground.

But that's just the soldiers who died fighting for the Union cause. Confederate bodies remained buried on the battlefield where they fell, unembalmed, covered, if at all, with only the tattered blankets they slept under in life, or the uniform they wore when they were slain, in unconsecrated graves, until the early 1870s. Unionists did not feel it was right to bury the Confederates in the same cemetery as the men they may have killed, so southerners remained buried out on the battlefield.

After the war the South was destitute. Because of the cost of the war and policies under reconstruction, they could barely afford to feed their families, let alone to bring the bodies of their dead husbands, brothers, and sons home for burial in southern soil. Not until groups of southern women, "Ladies' Memorial Associations," finally began to negotiate with local Gettysburgians who had done the original exhumation and reburial work on the Union soldiers did dead southern soldiers get attention. The Weavers—father Samuel and son Dr. Rufus—while they were exhuming the Union dead, had kept records of the locations of *all* burials on the field and were familiar with where the Confederates were buried.

Location and exhumation of Confederate bodies was begun in the summer of 1871. For three years, while the weather permitted, Dr. Rufus Weaver, who had inherited the burial records from his father, eventually collected some 3,320 remains and shipped them to the various ladies' societies across the South, with the largest number, 2,935, going to Richmond, former capital of the Confederacy.

It seems incredible that Weaver was able to locate and remove so many bodies. It has to be conceded that he did not remove *all* the Confederates, and that many still remained buried—like the most recent Union soldier's remains found in 1996—on the battlefield. Gregory A. Coco, in his book *Wasted Valor: The Confederate Dead at Gettysburg,* another exhaustive study of the aftermath of the battle, reasoned that since it was known that between 4,500 and 5,000 Confederates died in the battle and Weaver removed about 3,400, that probably some 1,500 remains have never been recovered.

Paranormalists will cite several reasons why a place may be haunted. Burial in an unconsecrated grave and disturbing a body's resting place are two. So it is fruitless to request a room in the newer section of a property because it won't be haunted.

It was the second (or perhaps the third) innkeeper who invited my team to do an extensive overnight paranormal investigation, since there had been a number of weird and unexplainable events. Historically, other than troops moving along some of the nearby roads, there was no battle fought on the grounds, but, no doubt, by its vicinity to so many field hospitals, plenty of death. But dead soldiers were not who we were destined to run into that night.

There was only one request: "Bring a couple of blondes." Apparently, whoever the entity was acted up more in the presence of blondes. Based on my knowledge of previous owners, the comment also gave me a clue as to who one of the entities might be.

The first blonde to round up was easy. Carol, my wife, (née Erickson) is of Scandinavian descent and is a natural blonde. Katherine Ramsland, my co-author on *Blood & Ghosts,* and *Haunted Crime Scenes* was in Gettysburg and is another blonde. She's an experienced paranormal investigator and wanted to spend another night in a haunted inn (having already spent the night and done an investigation at the Lizzie Borden House in Fall River, Massachusetts), so she was invited. And finally, we invited

Julie, one of the "spirit liaisons" we work with to come along. Julie is also blonde.

We arrived about dusk. It was the off-season, so the inn was empty, except for another paranormal group who had rented several of the rooms for the night. When we first arrived we explored the inn with the owner. Although I was very familiar with the downstairs, it was the first time I had an opportunity to visit the upstairs, which had always been the living quarters of the owners or occupied by guests of the inn. The other investigators were ones we knew well and whose work we respected. After the tour, we separated, some going outside to explore the grounds, others picking rooms to investigate.

Carol, Julie, Katherine and I ended up in this rather smallish room with two twin beds and a couple of chairs, one near the window. I let the blondes conduct the investigation. I sat in the chair by the window and took the roles of observer and recorder for the session: taking pictures and recording the session on a digital recorder.

At first there were people from the other group in the room. I took some random photos, especially of Julie. Often mediums attract unusual energies: orbs, paranormal mists, strange faces peering through windows, apparently interested in what they are doing. Sometimes, depending upon the otherworldly entities, it can get pretty hairy.

For example, Ron Kolek, a fellow investigator from New England came to Gettysburg. I had set up an investigation for him at the Daniel Lady Farm. Maureen, his friend, was a medium and was capable of "channeling" spirits or their energies.

Channeling is when the medium allows the spirit to enter his or her body to speak or communicate through. Remember, any speech-making apparatus belonging to an entity—larynx, tongue, lungs—has long ago decomposed, so they must "borrow" those things to communicate. Often, such as when using automatic writing, the medium's handwriting will change as the spirit communicates through the writing. When the spirit uses the body of the medium, the medium's voice may change: a female medium will begin to speak in a deep, male voice. The mediums lose themselves to the spirit, which seems to take over to get their point across. For the observer, it is unnerving to say the least.

At the Lady farm the group had entered the front room of the house, identified by location and bloodstains as the one used as the operating room by the surgeons. Wounded men were packed along the walls, some sitting when they could find some room, others standing. The line went out into the hall. The worst part is that those who were to be on the operating table watched as those before them had limbs shorn from their bodies, screamed when the surgeons ran out of pain killers, and had to be held down by orderlies as the surgery continued. They saw the surgeons rinse their hands in bloody buckets of water, wipe off their instruments with dirty cloths, and signal for the next patient.

As soon as she entered the room, Maureen backed into a corner. Her eyes changed into slitted, fearful features on her face, now contorted into a panicked countenance. She began muttering, then screaming and fighting invisible hands trying to grab her. She apparently was channeling the next soldier who was to lie on the operating table and was strenuously refusing to cooperate. The fighting grew violent, and after a few seconds, Ron, the leader of the group, afraid Maureen might fall and hurt herself, asked some people to help him hold her and calm her down.

I was videotaping the incident and was torn whether I should put down the camera and step in or continue to document the remarkable scene. Others began to step in to help Ron, so I continued to videotape, feeling strangely protected by the objectiveness of the camera. Maureen fought off the living, along with the invisible entities trying to drag her to the center of the room.

Her voice changed into the low-toned screaming of a desperate young man. Her strength grew as well, from a female paranormal investigator into a young man whose muscles had been toned from months of marching the roads to Gettysburg. It took several people to finally subdue her. Slowly the spirit who had used her left her body and she collapsed, exhausted after her struggle.

One of the other mediums who had been in the room said that, once Maureen had been taken over, she saw other spirits, like so many sharks, circling the room and attempting to enter the other people there. She said she had seen them try to enter me and bounce off.

(Only slightly more frightening on a personal level was the night Julie told me that while I was conducting a session to gather EVP, she saw the spirits taking energy from my spine. No wonder I am exhausted after every EVP session.)

Back to Julie's experience. I had been trying to get some EVP, addressing one of the former owners of the house, who, as I remembered seemed to enjoy the company of women, especially blondes. Could he be the entity still occupying his old house? Along with blondes, I knew he enjoyed his bourbon and I told him I was drinking bourbon at his house, just like the old days. I told him that I missed him. Upon replay of the recording, other than some white noise type background mumblings, I couldn't make out anything clearly. Then I asked a question: "Do they have bourbon in heaven?" and I got a rousing, loud noise, seemingly confirmation that one of my favorite past times may still be available in the afterlife.

A paranormal investigation can be a little frustrating because much of the data that is captured isn't discovered or recognized until you put it on a computer screen to enlarge it (as in photos) or run it through a computer audio program using earphones (for captured EVP). So I was resigned to the fact that it would probably be a pretty uneventful evening until I got back to my computer.

I was wrong.

About halfway through the investigation Julie made contact with an entity, apparently not associated with the house. According to the experts, occasionally we pick up psychic "hitchhikers"—entities that attach themselves to us for a while. Apparently, Katherine had brought an attachment with her. Julie was aware of its presence and decided to find out what it wanted.

I recorded the session in several two to three minute segments to make it easier to listen to later on. I had finished taking photos and was sitting recording and watching what was going on. Julie was facing a wall with a closet in it and Carol and Katherine were behind her sitting on one of the twin beds observing. Suddenly I heard Julie exclaim, "No. He's too far to the left. Too far to the left," and raised her arms as if fending off something I couldn't see. She continued to mumble something incoherent, seemed to become unconscious of her surroundings, and began to fall.

Julie was, by far, the tallest and largest of the three women in the room. She's a good four or five inches taller than Carol and much larger than diminutive Katherine. As I saw her start to stagger backward, I started to rise to catch her. But I was all the way across the room; there was no way I'd reach her in time.

As I watched, Carol and Katherine stood up to try and catch Julie, but instead of falling backwards and taking the two women with her to the floor, her body did the unbelievable.

She floated.

Her body *levitated* gently back into Carol's and Katherine's hands and the two women, using less energy than if they were carrying a blanket, moved Julie the few feet until she was over the bed then laid her down on it.

I sat back down in the chair, obviously not needed to prevent Julie from falling. I was astounded at what I'd just seen. Sometime after that I asked Carol and Katherine what happened. "She floated, she levitated," they said, and their efforts at placing her on the bed were minimal.

After several minutes, Julie "came to," oblivious to what had just happened to her.

As I said, much of the results of a paranormal investigation are not revealed until the analysis phase after the investigation venue has been vacated. This visual and physical evidence was immediate. Upon later analysis, more evidence of the bizarre night we spent surfaced.

I was going through my photographs and found one that couldn't have possibly been taken.

It was Julie, in the corner of the room next to the closet door, backed up almost to the wall with her elbow touching the corner. Because of the distance between the wall and the closet door, it is easy to estimate she was only between two and three inches from the wall. The odd part about the picture is that you can see a form standing behind her. A patterned shirtsleeve can be seen just under her blue and gray sweater's right sleeve, and a torso wearing the same shirt is seen behind her left side. It gets still more bizarre than just the fact that no one could possibly have fit in the three-inch space between her back and the wall.

It's my shirt. The one I was wearing.

I was across the room sitting in the chair. Or, I may even have been standing taking the picture. But it wasn't me behind her.

But it was my shirt.

Or, perhaps, as some have suggested, a supernatural prankster was replicating my shirt. Weeks later, we returned to the room and tried to reenact the photo. Needless to say, I could not squeeze into the three-inch space behind Julie.

That said, it gets even stranger.

I was reviewing the audio from the session after downloading it to my computer. There was one recording that caught my attention.

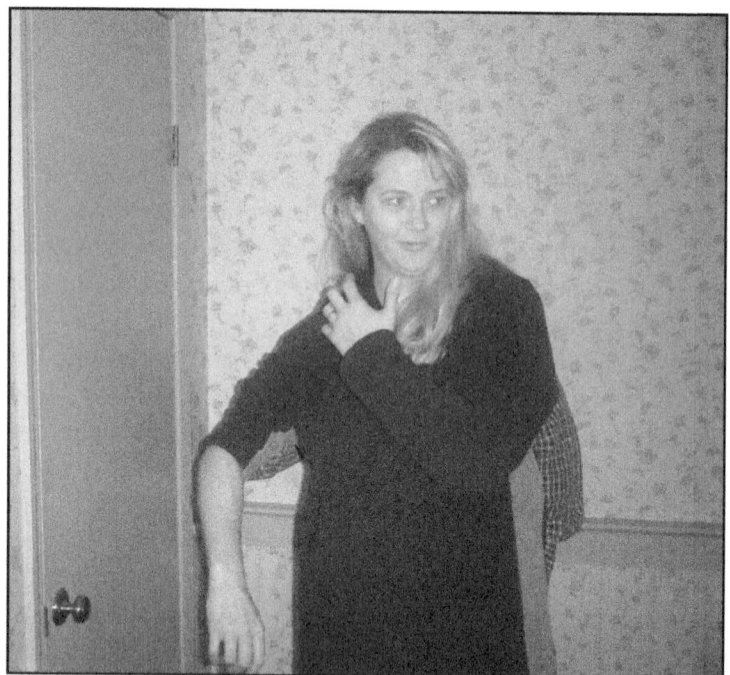

Julie at the Baladerry Inn

    It was a low-pitched, sing-song baritone voice, seemingly mocking, in an almost childlike tune. Whatever was happening in the room that night, I can't say for sure, but we had evidently been visited by something not benevolent or understanding. I can't say anymore about it than that, since I'm not versed in anything besides friendly or at least neutral spirits.

    The voice or noise I heard was menacing. I hope to never hear anything like it again.

THROUGH A GLASS, DARKLY

...you and I are going home today, and by a trail that is strange to us both.

—Half Yellow Face,
Crow scout to George Armstrong Custer,
veteran of Gettysburg, just before the
Battle of the Little Big Horn, June 25, 1876.

According to scientist Rupert Sheldrake, the definition of a premonition is a warning in advance; of presentiment is feeling in advance; and of precognition is knowing in advance. In paranormal terms, no matter what form it takes, it's the absolute certainty that something is going to happen in the near future. And all of these apply to the strange predictions documented before the Battle of Gettysburg.

Precognition has been used since ancient times, especially by "The Oracles," mystical individuals who, for one debated reason or another, were able to assist people in making decisions about their future. The most striking examples are when the Oracles helped generals devise tactics for their next battle. The most famous of these were the Oracles at Delphi. Their predictions were most often garbled and open to incredibly creative interpretation. Kings and generals in antiquity often used them, relying on information that seemed helpful, only to find out how disastrously wrong the Oracles were.

But perhaps no precognitive accounts—premonitions—are as striking as those that occur to individual average soldiers about to enter battle.

No doubt many—if not most—individuals headed into mortal combat have doubts about their survival. It only makes sense. With shot and shell flying and bursting in the air, the wicked bayonets of the enemy seemingly pointed right at you, and all the technology of a nation poured into the weapons aimed at you. In modern warfare, air-dropped bombs, rapid-fire machine guns, fiery napalm, land mines, IEDs, unseen underwater weapons, and the ultimate potential for nuclear weaponry, the odds of survival for the individual soldier may seem incredibly remote. Premonitions of death must happen frequently.

But more often than not, premonitions of death, expressed or kept to oneself, do not come true.

The same can be said for those soldiers who imagined their upcoming demise in the great Battle of Gettysburg unfolding before them in July 1863. Many believed with their whole hearts that this would be their last battle. Many of them survived it. But there were those who heard the same toll of the doomsday bell... and died.

On the morning of July 2, 1863, in the Georgia town of Americus (just a dozen miles or so from the infamous Confederate prison Andersonville), Mrs. David Winn strolled into her parlor and saw that one of the pictures that had hung on her wall had fallen to the floor. On the way down it had struck a chair. When she turned it over she drew in a horrified breath: it was a portrait of her husband, Lt. Col. David R. E. Winn, who was commanding the 4th Georgia Regiment. The chair post had pierced the Colonel's face. Mrs. Winn panicked and ran to her neighbor. There she confessed that at that moment she was certain that her husband had been killed in battle. The neighbors, of course, tried to calm her down. It was just a coincidence, no doubt. She calmed somewhat and got back to her housekeeping. Then, a few days later, Americus got the news of a huge battle on Pennsylvania soil near Gettysburg. When the casualty lists arrived in Americus, there, in the list of those killed in action, was the name of Lt. Col. Winn, slain leading his men in battle.

He had been shot in the face.

But it would be years before Mrs. Winn would have the comfort of having her husband's remains returned to his native soil where she could visit his grave and properly mourn her loss. While Union soldiers' bodies were gathered together shortly after the battle and respectfully buried in the new "National Cemetery"—dedicated by President Lincoln November 19, 1863—southerners' remains lay where they were hastily interred, scattered around the fields where they had died until the early 1870s.

As early as April 1864, the local Gettysburg newspaper printed a rumor that the fields where Confederate bodies were buried were about to be plowed up. The rumor was repeated in 1871, in a Georgia newspaper, and that the bones of Confederate dead, when found, were to be ground up for fertilizer. Articles like these seemed to spur southerners to make contacts in Gettysburg to have their soldier's remains exhumed and sent home.

They were usually packed several to a crate and sent to depots in Raleigh, North Carolina, Charleston, South Carolina, Savannah, Georgia, Richmond, Virginia, and Maryland. Some 73 separate boxes were sent to individual families, including one to Mrs. Colonel David R. E. Winn. Except for one thing.

Many Gettysburg area farmers had decided that for their "upkeep" of the graves on their properties, they were owed, often attempting to charge in advance for allowing the bodies to be removed from their land. (One must ask, were some of these farmers related to those locals who removed the handles to their well-pumps, then charged even Union soldiers who had been wounded defending their land from the rebels, a dollar to rent the pump handles so they might get a drink?) A map in Gregory Coco's, *A Strange and Blighted Land, Gettysburg: The Aftermath of a Battle* shows the farm of David Blocher north of Gettysburg, between the Carlisle Road and Blocher's Hill (now known as Barlow's Knoll). Just north of it is marked the grave of Col. Winn. Indeed, it was David Blocher's son with whom Dr. Weaver had to have somewhat gruesome negotiations for the lower jawbone, which contained a gold plate, of Col. Winn. Five dollars bought the ghoulish relic that was then sent to Mrs. Winn. After already waiting eight years for what remained of the body of her husband, that his jawbone should arrive separately due to the greed of a Gettysburg farmer seems inhumane in the extreme.

It seems at Gettysburg, Georgians were prone to premonitions. The 2nd Georgia was part of Benning's Brigade as it attacked from Seminary Ridge through the famous Triangular Field toward Little Round Top. Lt. Col. William T. Harris commanded the regiment. As they were preparing for the assault, Harris gathered some of his comrades from the regiment. He wanted to express a last sentiment to them for their friendship. No doubt they wondered why. He told them that he knew he wasn't going to survive the coming battle and wanted to say goodbye.

Shocked, saddened, and not wanting to believe it, they returned to their respective commands to await the orders to advance. Once they came, they saw that Harris had mounted his horse and was riding in advance of the battle line.

They crossed the fields and passed the farm of the Bushman family. As they did so, Union artillery on Houck's Ridge above Devil's Den opened on them with plunging shot. Still Harris and his men advanced.

They got to the Triangular Field just below the guns of Smith's Battery now firing anti-personnel rounds—canister and exploding shell—and Harris's horse was shot and killed underneath him. Harris leapt to the ground over his horse's head, drew his sword and continued to lead the 2nd Georgia on foot. Just as they were crossing Plum Run and entering the gorge it made through Devil's Den, Harris was shot down, still twenty yards ahead of his men.

Another Georgian's premonition came true.

One of the more famous incidents of precognition was the premonition of Col. Edward E. Cross of New Hampshire. As a young man he had worked his way up in the printing business to become editor of two newspapers in Cincinnati, Ohio, then got into the mining industry in Arizona. He possessed a fiery temperament illustrated by the fact that he fought two duels—one with rifles, the other with swords—survived them both and went to Mexico to join their army. In 1861, as Civil War broke out in America, he returned to New Hampshire to command their 5th Regiment of Volunteers. Soon he became commander of the First Brigade. Somewhat of a martinet, if his men didn't love him, they at least respected him and his ability to make good soldiers out of them. After two years of war, he found himself literally on the road to an upcoming battle and had an uneasy feeling about it.

Apparently, he had had these feelings before, but never to such an extent. On June 28, the brigade was encamped near Monocacy Junction, Maryland. Cross called Lt. Charles A. Hale from his staff closer and asked him to take care of his effects after he was killed. The next day he mentioned it again. Hale tried to ignore Cross's requests which only angered the Colonel. Still again, on July 2, Cross talked to Hale about the disposition of his belongings after they had crossed the Maryland-Pennsylvania line as they marched to the firing south of the town of Gettysburg. Again Hale tried to dismiss his colonel's frightening premonition. It was as they were preparing to go into the fight in a wheatfield—to be christened with blood as "*The Wheatfield*"—that Hale began to take Cross seriously.

As part of his pre-battle ritual, Hale had known Cross to tie a red silk bandana around his head, apparently so he could be identified by his men as their leader when he removed his hat. This day Hale was shocked to see Cross completely change his routine: today, around his head, Cross tied a black bandana.

Hale may have been even more frightened by Cross's exchange with Maj. Gen. Hancock, Commander of the Second Corps under which Cross's Brigade fought.

Hancock rode up and addressed the fact that after all the battles in which he'd been engaged, Cross was still a colonel. Hancock may have also realized the gravity of the upcoming fight that could stem the Confederate onslaught towards the left-center of the Union line.

"Colonel Cross," Hancock said over the rumblings of mortal combat just a few hundred yards away, "this day will bring you a star," indicating Hancock intended, after the fight, to promote Cross from colonel to brigadier-general.

"No, General, this is my last battle," Cross morosely replied. Hancock rode off and Cross rode into the Wheatfield toward his fate. Dismounting in the field of wheat, he walked into some woods behind his old 5th New Hampshire to get a better look at the enemy. One of them saw him first. A rifle belched fire and lead from a boulder only 45 yards from Cross. He took the soft lead, .58 caliber minié ball in the gut. The commander of the 5th saw the sharpshooter duck behind the rock and told one of his men to take him out. Cross's killer had only a few more seconds to live before he too was dead.

Cross died believing his men would miss him; he, no doubt, made a believer out of all those who doubted his precognition.

On the afternoon of July 2, there was a race for the summit of a hill on the south end of the field, later known as Little Round Top, between the Confederates advancing through the Plum Run Gorge, through Devil's Den and over Big Round Top, and Col. Strong Vincent's Brigade, rushing up the slope from the opposite direction.

Vincent's men, from Michigan, Pennsylvania, New York and Maine, won the sprint and fanned out along the southern and western slopes of the hill. As soon as the regiments got into position they sent out companies to spread out as skirmishers to warn of any approaching enemy.

Little Round Top

For the 44th New York went Company B under Capt. Lucius S. Larrabee. With a morbid curiosity, the men may have watched Larrabee more closely than the others in the company. As soon as they had arrived upon the field earlier that day, he confided in two other captains. He had given his watch and other personal items to the regimental quartermaster for safekeeping; he didn't want his body robbed of them when he was killed. Of the fact of his own impending death he was utterly convinced, and told his comrades. They tried to comfort him: the odds were certainly with him since the regiment, although blooded in numerous battles, had not yet lost an officer killed in action. Larrabee could not be dissuaded of what he believed was his doom. As his company set out for the skirmish line he bade farewell to one of the other captains who had wished him good luck: "Good bye, Billy. I shall never see you again."

Capt. Larrabee and Company B advanced a couple hundred yards, ran into a large body of Texans and began to withdraw back to the main line as was standard procedure for those soldiers acting as skirmishers. During the withdrawal one of the Texans lifted his rifle, brought it to bear on a Union officer, and Capt. Larrabee's premonition of his own demise came true.

Little Round Top, as both sides began to appreciate its strategic importance as one of the keys to the entire Union line, now began to act like a magnet for troops of both armies. In addition to infantry units, the Union Army ordered artillery to the summit.

Coming from the valley below Little Round Top was Lt. Charles E. Hazlett's Battery D, Fifth U. S. Artillery. Hazlett's Battery was given the position in the lead of the Fifth Corps artillery as they made their way down the Union line toward the fighting. Capt. Augustus P. Martin, commander of the Corps artillery recalled that Hazlett didn't want to be in the lead, that he would rather another battery head the column. It appears that he had recently received some unwelcome news from his family back home. From that news he drew a portent, a premonition that this would be the battle in which he would be killed. Martin denied Hazlett's request, wanted his special skills where he was headed, and therefore, inadvertently, set Hazlett on a course straight to his doom.

From the woods near the Trostle Farm, Martin and Hazlett galloped ahead of their artillery to locate good artillery positions. To them it was obvious: some artillery was needed on the high, bald hill to the east—Little Round Top—so Hazlett's battery was ordered there.

They rode to the crest, ran into Maj. Gen. Warren watching the battle from the hill, and all of them realized that it was not ideally suited for artillery. The summit was a narrow ridgeback—the guns could only line up facing west. As well, cannon could not be depressed enough to fire on an enemy who got close. The route up for the wheeled artillery was rocky; the route on the sheltered east side was wooded, virtually impossible for horses to haul cannons and caissons over. And all sides were steep—the animals would certainly need human help to carry the load. Even Gen. Warren—an engineer—didn't think the hill suitable for artillery. Hazlett argued that, if nothing else, the sound of his guns firing from such a lofty position would give the Union men below inspiration and discourage the enemy. Martin agreed.

The cannoneers drove the horses until close to the crest where they finally ran out of steam. Only one gun made it to the top under horsepower; the rest were wrestled to the top by sheer manpower, gunners and infantrymen alike lifting the half-ton pieces over stumps and stones, jockeying around trees, wrangling the guns, ammunition and equipment in the July afternoon heat until they were in position at the summit. Some of the sweating, swearing gunners bumped shoulders with a new man and looked wide-eyed as Maj. Gen. Warren himself leaned his sword against a tree and heaved with the privates and corporals.

Hazlett appeared, mounted on his horse, waving and pointing his sword where he wanted his guns positioned. Meantime, bullets—"a desperate storm of bullets" according to a witness—whistled past him. Before long, Hazlett's battery was firing from the summit of one of the keys to the battlefield.

It was hard work for the gunners, hauling the ammunition uphill from below the rear crest, then hauling the guns back into place after recoil every time a round was fired. They were also on the geological crest of the hill, not the military crest. The "military" crest of a hill is either slightly behind the geological crest so that the men could at least use the hill for some kind of cover, or, just down the front slope a few yards so they wouldn't be silhouetted on the skyline as easy targets. But the crest of Little Round Top is so narrow that Hazlett's men had no choice. As well, the rocky nature of the crest did not allow them to built lunettes—crescent-shaped mounds of earth—in front of the guns that were loaded through the muzzles, to protect the gunners as they moved to the front of the cannon to load.

In the meantime, Brig. Gen. Stephen H. Weed's brigade of infantry was also on its way to Little Round Top as Confederates overran Devil's Den and Big Round Top and were attacking the Union left flank. Just as some of Weed's men arrived at the summit of Little Round Top, they were thrown into battle with Confederates already on their way up the slope, and drove them back.

The rest of Weed's brigade spread out just below the crest, but in the growing dusk, the fighting had moved to the Wheatfield as Confederates secured Devil's Den and Union troops advanced into the valley below Little Round Top. Officers, including Weed and Martin, watched from the summit of Little Round Top, their position now seeming majestic as the sun began to creep toward the Blue Ridge Mountains on the horizon. Weed waxed poetic to his companion: "Martin I would rather die on this spot than see those rascals gain one inch of ground." Perhaps suddenly aware of the gravity of what might have seemed to him a premonition, Weed began assigning command duties to subordinates in case he was shot.

Martin had walked off to find Maj. Gen. Sykes, also on Little Round Top, but for some reason turned back to look at Weed just in time to see him tumble forward between Hazlett's guns. A lieutenant in the battery went to him and found him shot and paralyzed from the shoulders down. "I am cut in two," he said, no doubt expressing the strange feeling of his lower body seemingly separated from his upper. "I want to see Hazlett."

The lieutenant sent for him. Hazlett dismounted and leaned over Weed to get some last words assigning the payment of a debt to Hazlett. Then Weed pulled Hazlett closer to him, apparently to pass on a more private message. The gesture sealed Hazlett's fate.

Some nearby heard the hollow thud. Most saw Hazlett nose-dive over Weed's body, his brain destroyed by the entry of a Confederate minié ball. Both were probably shot by a sharpshooter lodged in Devil's Den. There's the likely possibility they were shot by the same Confederate who had the exact range and windage for that spot. Weed (still alive) and Hazlett (also still alive, but insensible) were carried to the field hospital behind Little Round Top and became two of the several mortally wounded Union officers brought to the Weikert's stone farmhouse on the Taneytown Road. In his dying hours, Weed was attended to by teenaged Tillie Pierce, the Gettysburg girl whose parents had sent her out of town for her safety when the battle roared by their doorstep. Ironically, she ended up behind Little Round Top in the Weikert field hospital. As she was leaving, Weed made her promise to see him the next morning in the Weikert's cellar where he was taken. When she returned, he was dead.

View from Devil's Den to Little Round Top

As a young park ranger I was told that one of the historians had triangulated the spot where Hazlett and Weed were shot with Devil's Den. The distance turned out to be 550 yards, proving that Civil War era rifled muskets were primitive only because of the loading procedures. Obviously, as the deaths of Weed and Hazlett show, in the hands of a skilled, experienced marksman, they were every bit as deadly as modern rifles.

While most of the regiments that fought on the Union side during the Civil War were volunteers, there were some professional soldiers. Many of these men had been in the United States Army when the war broke out, and probably would remain in it after the war against the rebellious states was over. These units were called the United States Regulars and at Gettysburg they fought in the Second Division in the Fifth Corps under division commander Brig. Gen. Romeyn Ayres.

As they stood in position just to the north of Little Round Top, J. P. Hackett, a soldier in the 17th United States Infantry, confident of their coming victory, teased his comrade Pvt. Sloan L. Cornell: "What hotel will you put up in tonight?"

According to Hackett, Cornell was "deathly pale" as he responded grimly, "I hope not in hell."

"Although there was no lack of firmness in his step," recalled Hackett years later, "I know now that he must have had a premonition of death."

As this day of death dragged on, the Regulars advanced from their position across the famous "Valley of Death"—the Plum Run valley—toward and into the Wheatfield to relieve Col. Cross's 5th New Hampshire and other units there. Confederate brigades advanced upon them in overwhelming numbers, interrupted their movement and began to drive them back. Hackett was elbow-to-elbow with a sergeant who took a bullet to the shoulder; aligning to the left on another company, Hackett sidled up next to Capt. William J. Moorhead who was struck by a bullet below the knee and tumbled forward, ordering his men as he fell, "Go on, boys." As if Hackett was being followed by the angel of death, he was next to his friend Sloan Cornell when Cornell took a one-ounce slug to the body just at the waist. He threw his arms around his friend's neck and said, "Oh, Hackett, I am killed."

Hackett hoisted Cornell in his arms and carried him back behind the battle line. He said that Cornell begged him not to leave him alone, but an officer reminded Hackett of his duty and he returned to the line, leaving his friend to die. Shortly, the entire brigade was ordered to retreat back to their original position, although to do so they had to pass through an area where they took fire from three directions at once.

It was years later in 1879, during testimony at the Warren Court of Inquiry in Washington, that Ayres was asked derisively by some politician concerning the actions of his men at the 1865 battle at Five Forks, Virginia, "Where were your regulars then?" Ayres gave the answer that spoke volumes about the dedication of and respect for the U. S. Regulars: "Buried, sir, at Gettysburg!"

Stannard's Vermont Brigade had been fortunate up to the Battle of Gettysburg. They had spent most of the war on easy duty, manning the defensive forts around Washington. But the Confederate invasion in the summer of 1863 forced the Union to strip the defenses of the capital, much to the chagrin of the politicians.

On July 3, before the grand assault from Longstreet's Corps known to history as "Pickett's Charge," a young corporal from the 14th Vermont Regiment left the ranks to visit his cousin just down the battle line in the 13th Vermont. The cousins had been boyhood chums in the pre-war years near Weybridge, Vermont. Cpl. Wesley C. Sturtevant met with Ralph O. Sturtevant never knowing what a pivotal role the entire Vermont Brigade would play in the battle in just a few hours. Once Pickett's columns struck the Federal line, the Vermonters, under Brig. Gen. George J. Stannard, would find themselves in an incredibly advantageous position.

But for the Sturtevant cousins, it was like old times...except for one thing. Wesley told Ralph about a dream he'd had sleeping on the battlefield just the night before. He tried to forget it until he realized its portent and took it as a sign he was not going to survive the coming battle. He didn't appear worried or frightened, just resigned to his fate. Ralph tried to break the mood. Surely he must be mistaken. But Wesley was convinced and there was nothing he could do but his duty. The boys parted.

When Pickett's men advanced across the broad plain to the west, the column must have looked unbeatable. It stretched nearly a mile wide—about the entire distance a Union soldier on Cemetery Ridge could see along the rebel lines—and was backed by several supporting columns. In all, some 12,500 southerners began the assault that would change the course of the war.

But right from the beginning they found themselves in trouble. Union artillery from Little Round Top spotted them and began firing as soon as the rebels broke from the woods on Seminary Ridge. The image of men "charging" at a sprint is misleading; the field of Pickett's Charge is nearly a mile wide. No man could be expected to run a mile then fight for his life. That would have to wait for the last fifty yards or so. The Confederates began the assault at a walk, the men shoulder-to-shoulder, in double lines with back-up forces behind to give depth and penetrating power to the attack. So the Yankee artillery had a field day. Some of the artillerists firing from Little Round Top said it was like a day at target practice.

Somewhere nearing the Emmitsburg Road, someone in the Confederate line "didn't get the word." The entire assaulting column was to begin a left oblique to angle toward the center of the Union line at a (now famous) copse of trees, which would mark the enemy line even above the smoke and haze from battle. Two Confederate brigades on their right flank continued moving in a forward direction while the rest of the assaulting column veered to the left.

The Confederate assaulting lines had inadvertently split just in front of the boys from the Green Mountain State, one Confederate column going just to their right, and the two other southern brigades meandering off to their left. Gen. Stannard saw the Confederate's tactical error and made them pay. He advanced the Vermont troops perpendicular to the rest of the Northern line and began firing volleys northward into the right flank of Pickett's main column headed toward the Copse of Trees. They loosed, by some accounts, eight or ten volleys, effectively destroying any support those men could give their center. It was a good thing—at least for the Union—because about that time Confederates under Brig. Gen. Lewis Armistead had broken through the center of the Federal line just north of the Copse.

Then, having wrecked that Confederate flank, Stannard's Vermonters did an "about face," advanced southward, and fired volleys into the left flank of the other wandering line of Confederates. It may have been *the* half hour of fighting that saved the Union at Gettysburg.

It was also about the only serious, stand-up fighting they did during the entire war.

On July 4, they were ordered to Baltimore, then to pursue Lee's retreating army, but were called off from that on July 8. They were ordered back to Vermont and, because of the end of their enlistment, were mustered out of the service on August 10, 1863.

Ironically, Wesley Sturtevant would not be mustered out with them. His dream premonition had come true. He was killed in the brief but important fighting of July 3, repelling the last Confederate assault at Gettysburg. He would eventually make it home to Vermont, however, in a casket. He was buried in New Haven, Vermont, under a stone carved with the inscription, "I have for my country fallen."

The vast scope of the Battle of Gettysburg may be the most misunderstood aspect of the history of the battle. People are amazed upon their first visit that they cannot climb a tower and look down at a field enclosed within a fence and in one sweep of the eye take in the site of the battle.

They fail to realize that the campaign, from early June to August 1863, took the Confederate Army from the Fredericksburg area of Virginia, west to the Shenandoah Valley, then north across Maryland and into Pennsylvania, with advanced forces, like tendrils, reaching as far west as Hancock, Maryland, as far north as the environs of Harrisburg, capital of the Keystone State, and as far east as the Susquehanna River. Add to that Jeb Stuart's cavalry sweep around the Union Army to the east, across the Potomac River, up through Maryland, north through Hanover, Pennsylvania, all the way to Carlisle where there was a U. S. Army barracks, fighting battles the whole way. The armies marched, cavalry scouts out in front covering every byway and cow path on either side of the main route searching out enemy ambushes.

So it shouldn't surprise anyone that, in addition to a large cavalry battle three miles to the east of Gettysburg, there was another near Fairfield, Pennsylvania, some seven miles to the west. The Confederate victory there would clear the way for the eventual Confederate retreat. It also supplies us with yet another example of the individual paranormal phenomena of premonition.

On the night of July 2, Lt. John Allan of the 6th Virginia Cavalry wrote a note: "Anyone who will deliver my body to Mr. Hoffman, my father-in-law, No. _____ St., Baltimore, MD, will receive the sum of $500." He carefully placed it in his pocket book. The next day, during the battle at Fairfield, Allan was shot from his saddle and killed, leaving behind a wife and two children. Pvt. John N. Opie and friends recovered their lieutenant's body and found the note in Allan's pocket book, written and dated just the night before. As the Confederates were retreating from Gettysburg, they left Allan's body and the promissory note with a civilian. Upon later inquiry, Opie found out that the request was honored and the money paid, fulfilling the premonition of the 31-year-old adjutant of the 6th Virginia. Allan was later buried in Shockoe Hill Cemetery, Richmond, Virginia. Opie claimed that this was just one of many instances during the war where a premonition of death had come true.

To add to the eerie nature of the paranormal phenomena experienced by Lt. Allan, his father happened to be John Allan, foster father of Edgar Allan Poe, the great American writer of the weird and supernatural and the Lieutenant's half brother by adoption.

Brickyard off Stratton Street on Coster Ave.

As well as stretching far and wide through the fields and hills around Gettysburg, the battle also raged in the town. On July 1, as Confederate troops drove Federal soldiers from their positions west, north and east of Gettysburg, fighting was conducted in the streets. A few pockets of Union troops fought rear guard actions. One brief battle took place at the crossroads of Chambersburg and Washington Streets; another larger fight occurred at a brickyard off Stratton Street and is commemorated by monuments, plaques, and a unique mural on Coster Avenue, which enters the east side of Stratton. There was a barricade thrown up by Confederates at the corner of Baltimore and Breckenridge Streets (in front of the *Ghosts of Gettysburg Tours* headquarters) to protect the Southern soldiers against fire from Union soldiers on Cemetery Ridge.

But Confederates apparently got even closer to the Union lines to pick off northern officers as they arranged their lines. Union commanders asked for volunteers to advance into the southern suburbs of Gettysburg to clear out the pesky (and deadly) rebel sharpshooters. One hundred men of the 82nd Illinois volunteered. Oddly, to the officer who commanded the patrol, Cpl. John Ackerman always one of the first in the unit to volunteer for any dangerous duty assigned the regiment, failed to come forward. The officer was so amazed at this uncharacteristic turn of events that he approached Ackerman and addressed him about it.

"Captain," said Ackerman, "I cannot go with you this time; I feel as though something terrible was going to happen to me today."

The captain wrote that Ackerman looked "pale and despondent." The captain thought perhaps he didn't feel well enough for duty. As he left, he said some encouraging words to him, and the rest of the volunteers moved out to clear the nearby houses of rebels.

Apparently, there is no escape from a premonition. Ackerman's experience seems to confirm the belief in pre-ordained fate and an inescapable doom. When the captain returned he discovered that just an hour after they had spoken, where Ackerman had remained in what he thought would be a place of safety, a Confederate shell had taken off half of his head killing him instantly. His comrades buried him on Cemetery Hill. Later, his remains were transferred to the Illinois plot in the National Cemetery, not far from where the premonition of his own death caught up with him.

THE GHOSTS OF SPRINGS AVENUE

To die will be an awfully big adventure.
— J. M. Barrie, *Peter Pan*

It would seem that one haunted spring of flowing water would be enough for a place the size of Gettysburg. Certainly, Spangler's Spring has its share of unexplained materializations, especially of a "woman in white" some have identified as a nun from a nearby convent. Alive, she and her sisters came from Emmitsburg, Maryland, a few miles south, when they heard of the horrific battle at Gettysburg, to care for the wounded. Dead, she apparently remains bound to her never ending duty of mercy, tending not to the physical, but to the phantom bodies of the slain around the spring named after the Spangler family.

But there was another spring that gained notoriety because of the battle and although the actual site of the spring is not known to be haunted for reasons that will be explained, locals along one of the routes to the site have reported strange, unexplainable happenings in their homes.

Sometime before 1830, Reverend Charles G. McLean discovered springs of mineral water on his land located just west of Willoughby Run and south of the road to Cashtown. Knowing mineral waters were beneficial to one's health, he attempted to interest some local Gettysburg individuals in partaking of the waters.

It took three decades and one of the greatest bloodlettings in American History before anyone took notice.

It wasn't until after the battle of Gettysburg, when rumors began to circulate of how the healing waters from the springs produced almost miraculous cures on the soldiers wounded around it on the first day of the battle that people began to take notice of the mineral springs to the west of town.

No doubt, the extraordinary healing powers were exaggerated, but by 1868, just five years after the battle, an organization called the Gettysburg Lithia Springs Association began to sell bottled water from the springs made famous by their rumored curative powers on wounded soldiers. By 1869, resort and spa buildings had been built for visitors attracted to the springs for their health benefits.

Springs Hotel from "Gettysburg: What to see, and how to see it." (Ninth ed.) by John B. Bachelder (1889)

The four-story wooden Springs Hotel featured a magnificent two-story cupola, a huge wrap-around porch, a large building in back along with a kitchen, large dining room, a "cotillion hall," separate parlors for men and women and a pool room. It was listed in 1893 as one of the leading hotels in Gettysburg.

A bridge was built over Willoughby Run, where Confederate soldiers once splashed across, to carry trolley tracks. A horse-drawn trolley brought guests from the Gettysburg Railroad Station, out "Springs Avenue," constructed specifically for that purpose, over the battlefields on Seminary Ridge to the "Katalysine Springs" hotel and spa. Along the trolley line was a roadway to accommodate carriages and other buildings were built along the road, thought to have been summer homes of investors in the project

The spa closed in the 1890s and the hotel went bankrupt by 1901. The 50th Anniversary of the Battle of Gettysburg in 1913 brought new life to the hotel structure when one entrepreneur purchased it specifically to rent accommodations to some of the large numbers of veterans expected to attend the festivities. After the anniversary, another attempt was made to fix up the building, which was spending more time abandoned than occupied. The renovations proved too costly and the immense structure was left to house just a single caretaker.

On December 17, 1917, just before noon, a fire broke out. The large hallways were blamed for helping to create a draft for the flames and the entire wooden structure was consumed in just half an hour.

Gettysburg Country Club

In 1948, the land that had been occupied by the Springs Hotel, spa, and adjunct structures was encompassed by a private golf course, which would later become the Gettysburg

Country Club. Its most famous golfer would be President Dwight D. Eisenhower. In the spring of 2011, the National Park Service acquired the country club land across which Confederate units attacked Union soldiers on July 1, 1863, during the opening phases of the three-day battle.

Though some historians believe that modern duffers may have taken divots where the bodies of unknown and forgotten soldiers lay buried, most of the ghost stories from the area come from the houses along Country Club Lane, Hospital Woods west of the Lane, and Springs Avenue. Perhaps golfers are too distracted to notice wispy figures floating across a fairway.

Though the trolley line is long gone, Springs Avenue remains as one of the more beautiful streets in Gettysburg. Broad, with beautifully kept large homes, Springs Avenue branches from Buford Avenue, past the old Meade School, now restored as a boutique hotel called the Federal Pointe Inn, up Seminary Ridge to the Lutheran Theological Seminary.

Yet the peacefulness of one of the lovelier residential areas in Gettysburg belies the fury of the conflict that once inundated the place. On the morning of July 1, 1863, Union troops of the First Corps, led by Maj. Gen. John F. Reynolds, rushed near the future vicinity of Springs Avenue over Seminary Ridge and directly into battle a few hundred yards beyond. Less than an hour later, Reynolds would be brought back along virtually the same route, a corpse. Within minutes of his arrival, he became the highest ranking Union officer to die.

Later in the afternoon, the Union lines, assailed from three sides, would collapse and their retreat turn into a rout as whooping, victorious Confederates would crest the ridge and swarm down upon them, all heading toward the center of town, then southward to Cemetery and Culp's Hills beyond the town. One must wonder, could it be the spectral remnant of some of the soldiers who expended so much energy to escape, then were slain for their efforts, that remains to bother some modern residents?

One family seemed particularly perturbed by unexplainable events in their Springs Avenue home. Lights in the house appear to be particularly affected. The entire family has noticed that certain lights will come on by themselves. Especially odd is a strange, eerie light in the basement. A family member will look into the cellar and see a light brighten, then dim. As they begin to descend into the cellar, it appears to be moving around, "floating" as some in the family have described it.

During renovations to the house, three family members were in the dining room. Some boards had been removed in the nearby closet floor and they could look straight down into the basement. The mother had the best view into the hole and was shocked at what she could see: a light "float" by the hole. Trying to relegate it to her imagination, she was resigned...until she saw it go by again. The others were concerned at her reaction, until they all saw it a third time. Shocked, frightened, not knowing what this mysterious light meant, they ran out of the house and locked the door. Once outside, their attention was drawn to the turret adorning the roof of the house. There, in the now empty house in the turret room, they all saw the shadow of man apparently watching them.

Though they've gotten used to sharing the house with the dead from another era, there are times when they will leave the house, checking to make sure all the lights are off, come back and find that pesky light in the basement on.

The mother reported that one time she was working on the floor with her back to the door and had that strange, but all too familiar feeling that someone was looking at her. She turned, expecting to see her husband or sons, but no one was there. At least not at first. She returned to her task, but within a few minutes felt it again. To her shock, out of the corner of her eye, she saw a man watching her. She stood to confront him, and he rudely vanished. Recently she was looking through some old books and was shocked to see the man looking back at her from the pages of photographs. He was a fairly well known historical figure from Gettysburg and the early Lutheran Seminary, the builder and original owner of the house. She is certain he is the man she saw watching her while she worked.

One of the sons was working on a ladder. At first he thought someone was playing a prank, because someone bumped him. Preparing to accuse his brother for such a dangerous joke, he was stopped short. A glance down revealed there was no one visible nearby. But it seems like nearly everyone who has worked on the house—plumbers, electricians, family members—has had something happen to them.

During the initial renovations to the house, electricians were working in the attic. Suddenly the lights went off. Professionals that they were, they checked the wiring, but their inspection only caused confusion: the wiring was fine. Suddenly, the lights went back on.

The grandmother of the family, who is adamant about her disbelief in ghosts, will no longer sleep in the house.

One of the sons revealed that several people who have visited have said that wherever they are in the house, it feels like there is someone looking at you. You are compelled to look over your shoulder the whole time you are there.

Even the family dogs are not immune. One of the dogs will stop in his tracks, seeing something no one else sees. He looks nervously back and forth from his owner to the spot where he apparently sees the invisible entity. There are a couple of rooms in the house that the dog absolutely refuses to go into.

They had just bought four brand new rocking chairs for the nice sized porch on the house. It was a pleasant evening with no breeze and family members were occupying two of the chairs on the porch. Suddenly, one of the empty chairs began rocking. It was as if the family members had been cordially joined in their relaxing evening rocking on the porch.

The woman of the house is adamant that they don't feel threatened. She even got an old photo of the man she saw peering at her as she worked and placed it on the mantle. She often politely says hello and goodbye to the image as she passes.

But they are not about to leave anytime soon. As if to demonstrate Carl Jung's phenomenon of synchronicity, one of the sons found some old books in the attic. By the inscriptions inside of them, two had belonged to his great grandmother. He questioned the family and they have absolutely no explanation how they could have gotten there.

And just so you don't think that ghostly phenomena are confined to this one family, just down the street is a house that had been broken up into apartments.

I was doing some research just outside of Gettysburg at a retail place of business. A woman who worked there casually mentioned that she lived on Springs Avenue and was having some "problems" with what she thought were ghosts. I told her I was working on a chapter about Springs Avenue for my next book and she related some strange happenings in yet another house on the lovely street.

As a reader can tell from my books, "seeing" a ghost is only one way to experience the paranormal at Gettysburg and other places. A rough estimate is that only about ten percent of all ghostly experiences are visual. It seems that all the human senses are affected, including smell.

The woman lives in the Springs Avenue house with her daughter. Both have smelled the distinctive odor of someone cooking when they are the only ones in the house at the time. The daughter one day said she smelled rotten eggs. This awful smell has been reported frequently in various parts of Gettysburg. Numerous individuals on our ghost tours have spoken of it, and reports from various parts of the battlefield confirm the odor of rotten eggs. The evil smell can possibly be attributed to the psychic remnant of the propellant for firearms during the Civil War, black powder, whose main ingredients were charcoal, saltpeter and sulfur. Anyone who has attended a modern reenactment has the unforgettable stench emblazoned on their olfactory nerves. Those who have visited the camps of reenactors no doubt have smelled it, for it embeds itself in the clothing. Those who have taken a chemistry class can certainly remember the rotten egg smell of sulfur. Second only to the smell of decomposing flesh, it was a predominant assault on the sense of smell long after the battle, permeating the air around the town.

But the activity extends into the realm of the poltergeist as well.

The daughter has witnessed on several occasions lights in the house flicking on and off all on their own. Like so many others being bothered by a poltergeist, she has watched as a door opened and closed, by itself.

It could be unnerving, being the target of a poltergeist. They seem to come from out of nowhere when you least expect them. It is bad enough to be frightened by a loud noise—someone dropping something on the floor or a housemate unexpectedly slamming a door. But when there is no one visible to do the action, it is nearly too much to take.

It was late one night. The woman had been in bed asleep with the lights off. She was awakened by a sound that should be familiar—footsteps coming across the floor. In the grogginess of being awakened, at first she relaxed, thinking it was just her daughter coming home after work. But then she realized something. Those weren't her daughter's light footfalls.

Her first impression was that it was the walk of a "strong man." Again she thought it was her daughter coming home with boots on. She yelled into the darkness, "Take those off!" and turned on the lights to confront her noisy daughter. Imagine the cold chill of fear when the room was illuminated and she realized—no one was there. Sleep came with great difficulty the rest of the night.

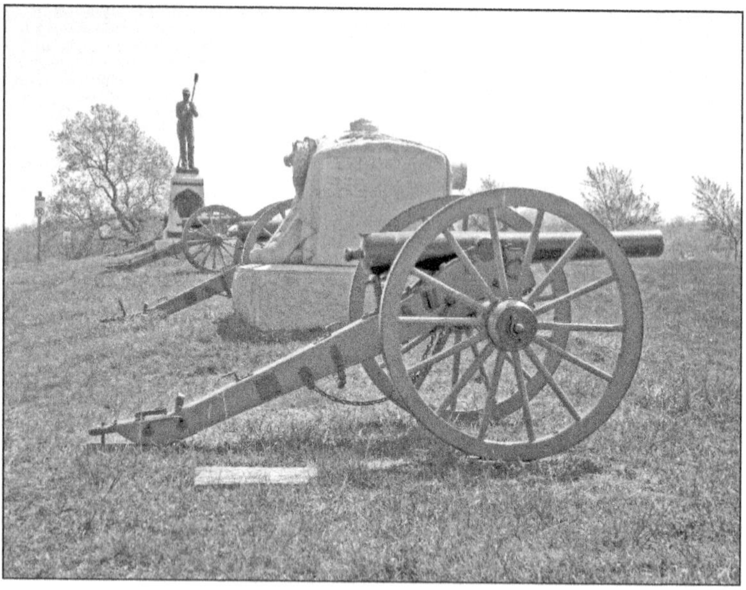

AGAIN, THE DEVIL'S DEN

Art thou some god, some angel, or some devil,
That mak'st my blood cold, and my hair to stare?
—William Shakespeare, *Julius Caesar*

Of all the battle sites throughout the Civil War—Bloody Pond at Shiloh, the Bloody Angle at Spotsylvania, Bloody Lane at Antietam, the Dead Angle at Kennesaw Mountain—none depicts the abject doom and despair implied by the pile of boulders at Gettysburg named Devil's Den.

To be bloodied is one thing; to die is another; to be associated at death with the Devil's home is another thing entirely, as if some past sinfulness has led one to one's demise in that particular place.

Devil's Den

It can be a forlorn place. In the daylight, not so much, with children playing on the rocks and the safety of vehicular escape yards away in the parking lots. Perhaps the only worry is whether one of the huge rocks, which has rested in that spot for a million or so years, will choose at that moment to tumble from its perch, just as you walk below it.

At night it is a different story. Gigantic, dark boulders loom menacingly above; cracks and fissures in the granite rocks hide un-named dangers; no one can really be sure what lurks just around the next dark corner; legends of the place seem to come alive at night.

Emmanuel Bushman, a 19th Century historian from Gettysburg, published an article in 1880, which mentioned "many unnatural and supernatural sights and sounds" coming from the area of Big and Little Round Top. In spite of the names given the sites by soldiers and historians, he still called them the "Indian Fields." Early settlers to the area, he wrote, had told tales of ghosts roaming the woods and among the rocks and of hearing what they called "war-whoops" echoing through the trees at night. This was recorded years after the last Native Americans had left what was to become the Gettysburg Battlefield.

He wrote again, in 1884, about a tribe having lived near what is now called Devil's Den and that he thought the massive boulders and rocks may have been part of a great pyramid that had been destroyed by some catastrophic blast which left its mark on the rocks.

How much of this tale was local folklore or a figment of Bushman's imagination that he recorded can only be speculated. The thought of gigantic pyramids built at Gettysburg was once laughable. That Native Americans used pyramids—like the ancient Egyptians—is undeniable; the evidence is in South America slowly being exposed as the tree cover is being peeled back. Research done on ancient Indian cultures in South America, their massive pyramids, and the questions as to how a primitive culture could have carved and moved the huge rocks to build them, makes Bushman's claim gain just a bit more credence.

I've often said that the most common ghostly phenomenon experienced at Gettysburg is auditory; "visuals,"—in other words, seeing a ghost—constitutes only about ten percent of all the stories I've collected. People will hear a ghost before they see one, and the most common of all unexplained noises is footsteps.

I heard them in the National Cemetery Lodge, coming down the stairs with no body—at least no *visible* body—accompanying the sound. A friend of mine heard a column of cavalry horses galloping down her dirt driveway one dark night. Where? East Cavalry Battlefield, of course.

And a series of stories I received over the years confirms that one place seems to harbor more peripatetic ghosts who reveal themselves with their footsteps than just about any other on the battlefield. I've written about footsteps and horses hooves being heard at Devil's Den. Its geographical neighbor, the Triangular Field, has its share of bizarre sounds and activity as well.

A man wrote to me about an experience he had with his girlfriend's family. He wrote that he had long been a Civil War buff, and just as long been a skeptic about the ghostly phenomena he had heard occurred at Gettysburg. His history teacher had told him the place was haunted; even showed him the evidence on the Internet. He remained unconvinced. It was his girlfriend who suggested they come to Gettysburg for a vacation.

Although he is a skeptic, he admitted that she was very sensitive to "the other side." Their first evening in Gettysburg, they visited Devil's Den and the Triangular Field, actually standing where they could observe both. After a few minutes of contemplative silence, his girlfriend pointed to an area and told him to take a picture with his new digital camera. Immediately he saw on the screen a veritable cloud of orb anomalies. Then she pointed to another spot and his photo again was filled with orbs. Every time she told him where to take a picture, the screen was crowded with the strange lights.

She also saw silhouettes of soldiers moving in the fields. They took one of our *Ghosts of Gettysburg Candlelight Walking Tours* that evening and she smelled pipe tobacco the entire time. She told him that she saw soldiers in the Twin Sycamores house, before the guide began her story about two of our tours seeing soldiers moving around in the house. She saw a lady (deceased) on the side porch of our headquarters house, before the tour even began.

They returned to Gettysburg a year later with her mother, grandmother and brother. The women in the family all exhibit "The Gift" as psychics call their supernatural talent. Visiting Devil's Den again in the evening, all the women saw silhouettes of different colors ranging from black to gray to white. Some were as solid as living beings; others were translucent. His girlfriend saw the heads of soldiers pop up, peeking from around boulders as if curious to determine whether these individuals were the enemy once more attempting to annihilate them. She saw them so clearly, she could make out individual faces.

They drove to Spangler's Spring near the foot of Culp's Hill. While there they were treated to the rattle of gunfire and the unnerving sounds of men screaming in pain coming from the hill (a phenomenon recorded in a previous *Ghosts of Gettysburg* volume). This time it wasn't just the women who experienced it; the writer heard it as well and admitted to the physical affirmation of goose bumps and the feeling of his hair standing on end. Then, just twenty yards from where they stood, he heard one long, loud scream and, although it was August, felt the paranormal chill flow through his body. Oddly, the "sensitives" in the group did not hear it.

They, apparently, were busy seeing figures moving around them. His girlfriend was about to take a picture when she felt a hand and all five fingers grasp her forearm. An icy cold wrapped around her arm where the hand was. Then it let go and her arm became exceedingly hot. As she stood there, someone unseen began tugging on her shirt to get her attention, an experience I once had during a night investigation of the Daniel Lady Farm. Although no one else was around, they smelled pipe tobacco and the odor of horses, which they knew from owning their own horses. By then it was nearing closing time in the Park and they headed back to their Bed and Breakfast, figuring that would be the end of their ghostly adventures.

How wrong they were.

They talked for a while about his first experience with the paranormal, then turned in. He admitted that he was tossing and turning, trying to sleep, when his girlfriend suddenly drew in her breath. He asked her what was wrong and she said there was a soldier at the foot of the bed. He continued to toss and turn until she was asleep. Then he felt two gentle taps on his shoulder. He rolled over, but his girlfriend was sound asleep facing the other direction. His interpretation was that the soldier was telling him that he wasn't to worry, to calm down and get some sleep. Suddenly his fears melted, thanks to the assurance from the other world, and he fell asleep.

I received a letter from a woman who grew up near Gettysburg, but moved away as an adult. Some of her relatives still lived in the area and I happened to know them. She said Col. Jacob M. Sheads had been her history teacher, but that it may have been something otherworldly that hooked her on Gettysburg. She put it in an odd way: her interest may have come from "before memory of this life." Because of recurring dreams as a small child that had to do with events she couldn't possibly have read about or known about, she was a believer in reincarnation.

She admitted that in high school she would go out on the battlefield at night. At Devil's Den she would often hear voices, but attributed it to unseen friends' voices echoing through the weird rock labyrinth. More than once she was startled by the sounds of people running through the Den, dozens of men, scrambling through the boulders. She rationalized by telling herself the noise was a herd of deer they had frightened. She never really convinced herself.

Occasionally she would pick up the rotten egg smell of gunpowder. She had convinced herself that it was her imagination...until she read my books and realized how many others had the same odor waft into their nostrils.

But what she called the weirdest experiences happened when she found a special rock she would sit on, her favorite place. When she sits there, things begin to change. She no longer hears the tourists chattering and shouting in the background; she says every sound becomes muffled and distorted, as if she was in an airplane and her ears are being affected by the altitude. She has seen, on a perfectly clear day, a haze settle over the field before her virtually every time she has visited that rock. Sometimes the muffled sound becomes a roaring in her ears, yet it disappears as suddenly as it had started. She always thought the experience lasted from ten to fifteen minutes. Once, she looked at her watch when the humming started. When the time passed and she looked again at her watch, only twelve seconds had elapsed.

I received another letter from a man who, along with his son and a number of friends, is a reenactor, officially sanctioned by the National Park Service to demonstrate and instruct on the park. They had finished for the day and were having their group dinner when they heard the distinct sound of artillery firing in the distance. Later, they checked with officials and were told that they must be mistaken—they were the only artillery reenactors on the field that day.

After dinner they decided to take a walk through Devil's Den and the Triangular Field. By then it was dusk, but they were not alone as they entered the Triangular Field.

First there were a number of tourists visiting the area. As the reenactors waited at the gate into the Triangular Field for a number of them to pass out of the field, one man asked them to say something to his wife to assure her they were alive and not ghosts.

As his son held the gate for the reenactors to enter the field, he suddenly said that he could feel someone holding his hand down on the gate. This could be debunked as the results of an active youthful imagination, except for the fact that as the reenactors put their hands close to the young man they could feel the area was at least thirty to forty degrees colder than the surrounding air. The young man began to feel the chill. His father said that all the color had flowed from his face and he turned white as snow.

Triangular Field Gate

There is a paranormal phenomenon called "Old Hag Syndrome," or sometimes "sleep paralysis." It usually only occurs when one is asleep, then wakes to find that he or she cannot move, as if some other body is pressing down upon them. Could this be what the young man felt pressing down on his hand for a few frightening moments?

After ten minutes of taking pictures they moved to the area of Devil's Den where Plum Run passes. The small creek drains the valley between Little Round Top and Hauck's Ridge and was named "Bloody Run" by the soldiers. For a few horrid hours in American History it literally ran red from the blood of the combatants in the area. Three of the group approached the stream, stepping off the road. Immediately their olfactory nerves were assaulted by the unmistakable stench of massive decomposition. Just ten yards away, the author of the letter, while standing on the modern roadway, could smell nothing. One must ask, if by stepping off the modern road, did the reenactors accidentally pass through a portal into the past?

Plum Run aka Bloody Run

I have written about the artist Jeff Prechtel before. He is a fine artist of the American past, concentrating on portraits of

Mountain Men and Native Americans. His research is impeccable and he often reenacts the era he paints. My first encounter with him was when he accompanied his father Don Prechtel—another great historical artist whose works hang at VMI and have been reproduced as fine art, limited edition prints—and we all had our cameras fail in the Triangular Field, legendary for its effect on electronic equipment.

Several years ago he was going through some photos he had taken from the Bloody Run area below Devil's Den. He remembers that they were alone that day, just one other couple in the parking lot. He took the picture from near where the old stone restroom building once stood, shooting toward where Joshua Chamberlain's 20th Maine's battle line ended. Looking at the photograph he noticed something he hadn't before. There, along a dark tree line, is what appears to be a line of soldiers. An enlargement of the color photo indeed shows a line of seven or eight heads packed tightly together, as if they were perhaps in two lines. They are wearing dark blue or indigo jackets and light sky blue pants, uniforms exactly like the Union soldiers wore during the battle. At least one of them appears to have a raised rifle about to fire. To their right, seemingly emerging from behind a tree is a slightly taller man dressed in light blue or gray with a light colored gauntlet on the hand that can be seen.

Another letter I found in my archives contained two photographs from a bizarre evening a woman and her husband experienced in the darkness of Devil's Den.

She had already conducted a "mini" investigation when her sister had them over to take pictures in her home after some strange happenings. With their 35mm cameras they captured hazy mists and vortexes in the highly active home. Later she bought her first digital camera and brought it to Gettysburg specifically to capture one of the ghosts of Gettysburg.

Crouching Soldier Statue

Driving through the battlefield at night can be a truly frightening experience. Shadows cast from headlights become dark soldiers ducking behind trees; trees suddenly illuminated by headlights coming over a hill loom as if they are alive and attacking; one particular monument—a crouching soldier—carved of white marble at a strategic bend in the road, appears to move as car lights scan across him. Stopping and getting out of the car on the battlefield at night, for those who only know a little about the bloody legacy of the ground upon which they walk, can be truly unnerving.

Once they got to Devil's Den, the woman realized that the battlefield was more eerie that she ever imagined it could be.

She and her husband met another family with two young girls and decided to investigate as a group. Using her husband's flashlight, they navigated the stone steps up into the Den. Once at the top, they all began to take photos. Suddenly one of the young girls said that her camera had stopped working. The other girl said that her flash had quit.

Their attention was drawn to her husband's flashlight, which began to slowly dim, then extinguished completely. They were in total darkness.

The young girls grew upset and started crying. The woman's new digital camera began to take on a life of its own. The device turned itself off. Then back on again. Then off again.

She recalled that she had charged the batteries just before coming out. It was virtually a brand new camera, so she was familiar with its operation having just read the directions. After reviewing everything she could about the camera, she never thought that it might not be the camera, but the subjects she was attempting to capture and the spot where she was trying to capture them that was causing the problem. Everyone gathered around to watch the camera turn itself on and off, on and off.

After a few minutes, the camera ceased its unexplainable activity and began to function properly again. The woman managed to take two pictures and they started back toward the parking lot having had enough of Devil's Den and its mischievous spirits. But the spirits weren't done with them yet.

By the time they reached the parking area, the flashlight's operation returned to normal. Looking at the pictures she took, she realized that, despite the fact that there was no fog and no one was smoking, she had captured that ropey, swirling, tangled mist paranormalists call ectoplasm. In one of the photos, the mist in the center top of the photo had formed into a face, replete with hollow eyes, cheekbones, nose, and what appeared to be a moustache. In the upper left hand corner is what appeared to be a round, cherubic face, tilted slightly to the right. Its right ear can be seen, as well as a broad upturned nose. The mouth, with finely shaped lips, was frozen open in a silent scream.

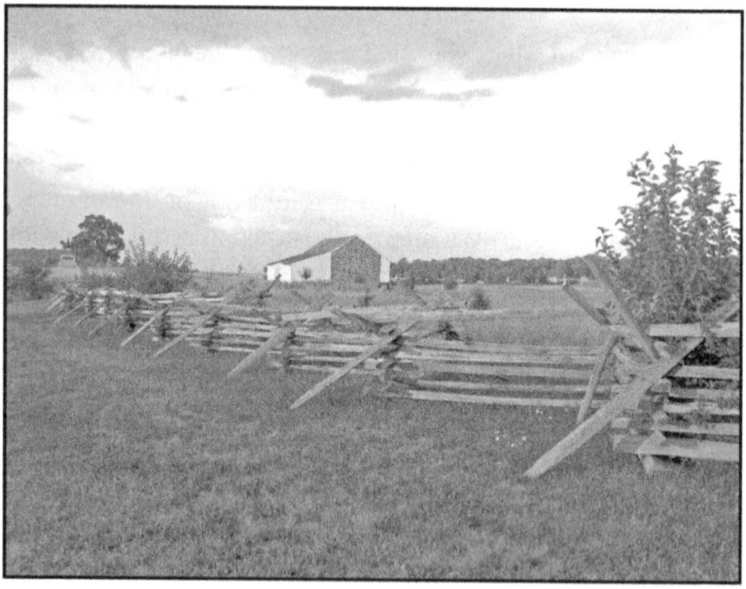

THE TRIANGULAR FIELD

"...remembering how his uncle had said that all man had was time, all that stood between him and the death he feared and abhorred was time yet he spent half of it inventing ways of getting the other half past."

—William Faulkner, *Intruder in the Dust*

Of all the day-to-day phenomena we have to deal with in our lifetimes, none is more familiar, confusing and less understood than time.

In spite of the fact that we are all aware of the passing of time as our day progresses and our years of life roll on, and the fact that time is omnipresent, like some all enveloping but invisible, odorless and tasteless gas, we can't get a handle on it. And, as I've written before, the only real reason time even matters, is because of death.

Some philosophers liken time to an arrow, moving inexorably in one direction and one direction only. But what we're interested in here is the malleability of time, how time warps or produces portals, so that we may see back through it. (Some even argue that there are people who can see forward through time, as in premonitions or prognostications—seeing the future.)

Many difficult aspects of science can be explained by using analogies or comparing the difficult with something simpler and more understandable. Perhaps our visualization of time needs to be altered. Instead of imagining time as an arrow always moving from now into the future, perhaps we should consider time as a fluid—like water—in motion.

Why not? We often refer to time as "passing," indicating we have imbued it in our minds with some kind of motion or energy. Time has already been thought of allegorically as a river, which gives it more familiar qualities than the arrow analogy.

There are moments when we feel that time is crawling along; others when it goes by too fast. Observe a river and you will see it change speed, too: where the banks are wide, the river flows slowly; other times the river banks narrow and hydraulics forces the water to rush through.

Floating objects move along relative to each other, either slowing or speeding up together, much like us and our acquaintances and possessions as we pass through the hours of the day or the years of life.

Beneath the surface, holes and other features in the riverbed affect the movement of the water and objects on the surface like unseen, invisible forces. The only way we can tell they even exist is by their effects on objects floating along the surface or by plumbing the depths of the stream.

Whorls are created as water passes around rocks, trees or other objects. Sometimes the water curls around the object and traps things behind the obstruction, leaving them to stop dead in the eddy created there, often for a long time. If time is thought of as a fluid, it could explain why things hang around for decades—or centuries, to finally be observed under certain conditions.

A fluid's non-compressibility could explain why time is inexorable and never stops moving.

The random combining of two waves in a larger body of water than a stream either cancels out their energy or increases it depending upon which direction they are moving when they combine. When two waves come together they can create a "super-wave" wielding incredible energy, sometimes upsetting or even destroying things currently associated with it.

Other phenomena produced by water may find their way analogously into time studies. Think of airborne spray, droplets, waves, troughs, ripples, colloidal suspension, buoyancy (or lack of it), mists, and evaporation. And the fact that in an encounter with water/time it leaves traces on participants.

Thinking of time as a fluid gives its strange behavior a location. While normally flowing smoothly, occasionally, at one particular physical spot, time is disrupted and reality as we perceive it is altered.

One such location may very well be the Triangular Field at Gettysburg.

Dale Kaczmarek has been investigating ghosts since 1975. He is the author of many books and articles on the paranormal and founder of the Ghost Research Society in Illinois. He is a paranormal researcher who takes a skeptical scientific approach to the field. Since our first sweep with instruments of the Triangular Field in the early 1990s, I have had profound respect for Dale and his work.

A few years ago we were scheduled to speak at a conference together, so I gave him a call to touch base. Just as I was about to hang up, he asked if he'd ever told me his most recent experience in the Triangular Field. I couldn't recall, so he told me of an experience he'd had that seems to fit in with others.

He was investigating the Triangular Field with a friend. They were going "old school" with just a few pieces of equipment, basically a video camera that would only light six to eight feet in front. It was dark and they were about to leave the area when they got a very strong odor of what they thought smelled like cherry pipe tobacco wafting down the field toward them. Within a few seconds they heard a horse clop-clopping along the park road above them. (The Park Service is very strict as to when and where horses may travel—on designated bridle trails, none of which go along that road, and certainly not at night.)

The horse sounds stopped abruptly. But then they saw a figure moving up the slope ahead of them. It moved without stumbling over the rough terrain, almost as if it was floating. They tried to follow it, but it always kept ahead of them, silhouetted along the skyline by the dim light from the south end of town. Though they followed and watched the figure until they got to the top of the field, by the time they reached the road, it was nowhere to be seen.

It was nearing 10:00 P.M., so they began to drive out to Route 15. The entire way they saw no other cars or any trace of the figure.

The next day they returned to the Triangular Field and inspected the area that was crossed by the figure. The path was blocked by a monument surrounded by thick briars, which would have been impossible for a living person to traverse.

Triangular Field

Another letter came from a woman who said that because of my books, she and her son were interested in visiting the Triangular Field.

It was between noon and 1:30 when they got to the oddly shaped, sloped field once fought over so viciously.

They walked down the field to experience what the Confederates had on their way back up. She recalled that they were the only ones there at the time and that it was a nice sunny day.

As they walked down the path her son made a curious remark. He said it sounded like bullets were whistling past his head. In an attempt to explain the odd sounds away, she blamed the bees and wasps flying by. Her son was not convinced.

At the bottom of the field and she spotted a large flat rock and decided to walk to it. They stood there by themselves for a minute or two when she heard what sounded like someone tramping through the grass nearby. She heard it, but the only other people were at the top of the hill by the gate and rock wall. What she was hearing seemed to come closer.

At first she tried to rationalize the sounds as rabbits, but listened more closely and realized that the footfalls were too heavy for a rabbit, and rhythmic, like someone marching. Not finding the source for the tramping sounds, they began heading back up the path. As they did she suddenly began hearing what her son had heard earlier: the sound of something heavy like bullets whistling past her head. She was convinced about what her son had heard. They were definitely not insects.

A couple of photos she had taken while in the field came out strangely. (Of course, the good news in the Triangular Field that day was that her camera worked at all!) The image of her son seemed like it had been pasted into the picture on a different layer than the background.

By the time they left the area, she had dismissed the sounds as the products of an over-active imagination. When they got home she read about the Triangular Field in one of my books. She believes that the rock they visited at the bottom of the field is the same one around which groups of soldiers have been videotaped.

A fellow paranormal investigator took a friend out to the Triangular Field one evening as part of my *Ghosts of Gettysburg Battlefield Tour* available as a download. It was the beginning of October around 8:45 P.M. They stopped in the parking area just past the park information signs. They got out of the car to listen to the tape through the open window and take in the silent, falling darkness of the battlefield. They soon got a little more than they had bargained for.

Almost immediately he saw an orb of light between a large rock and the skyline. A few seconds later a twig snapped in the bushes behind a fallen tree near the informational signs. Then another. They both heard it.

Then came the horses' hooves, clop-clopping along the road beyond the signs. Or at least what he thought at first were horseshoes. He wrote that they sounded metallic on the road like horseshoes, but were more regular like human footsteps. One thing was for sure: they were approaching in the darkness.

By now the footsteps were so close they could follow the sounds as they passed by the side of the car, steadily walking, walking, to the front of the car and onto the gravel of the parking area. They stopped just three feet in front of them and made a sound in the gravel as if whoever it was had turned to face them. He wrote that he knew by their sound where the footsteps were, but could see neither a figure nor the gravel moving.

While their attention was drawn to the sounds at the front of the car, suddenly they heard softer footsteps begin to approach them from behind. Soon he was convinced that they were being confronted by two entities, but couldn't see either one in the dusk.

He began to feel menaced and after a short time my investigator friend rushed around to her side of the car and re-entered. He tried to say, "We mean you no harm," but he couldn't get the words out and hurried to the safety of the car.

He lit a cigarette to calm himself and decided to repeat an experiment he had tried with success once before at Gettysburg. Some months back on the other side of the Valley of Death, he had lit a cigarette and, knowing the virtually universal use of tobacco during the Civil War, held it out and told the entities to go ahead and take a puff. To his astonishment, the burning end of the cigarette glowed brighter and smoke came out of the filter end. Now, again he held out the burning cigarette and offered a puff.

This night he had no takers.

A young woman wrote to me about her experiences in the Triangular Field. She explained that she was a Civil War buff going to Gettysburg College and while she had heard the ghost stories about the town, campus and battlefield, maintained a healthy skepticism. On one night in October, that skepticism was challenged to the max.

She and four friends got to Devil's Den about 8:00 in the evening. At that time in October, they needed flashlights to get around. After exploring the Den to their satisfaction, they wandered over to the adjacent Triangular Field, mainly because they had heard it was one of the more haunted sites on the battlefield.

They got fairly far out in that weird field, near the woods at the bottom, when they heard noises she described as if people were tramping in the woods. They turned on their flashlights, but they were no help: nothing was seen that could have made that kind of noise. But they kept hearing the noise, this time coming from all different directions.

They continued to walk when suddenly all of them noticed that the temperature had dropped significantly in the area they had just entered. They turned and looked back into the field and all saw a gray figure about sixty yards away. They agreed that it looked like it was in a crouched position. The worst part is that it was moving toward them.

They shined one of the flashlights on it, but the light passed through it. What they were able to discern was that it was human in shape and appeared to be wearing a dark gray coat.

As they peered at the figure trying to determine if they were in danger, another figure appeared about eighty yards behind it. This one, however, remained stationary. But to everyone's shock and horror, the first figure began running toward them. It got to within twenty yards before the group broke and ran for the road, escaping from whatever mischief the entity had in mind.

There is the persistent rumor of a huge Indian battle waged in the vicinity. One source placed the epic battle between two powerful tribes within a mile west of Big Round Top. Legend has it being at least as large as the battle fought by the white man in July 1863.

From almost my first day as a park ranger at Gettysburg, I remember someone talking about evidence that there had been a huge Native American battle near the Round Tops. Later, as I got to know some of the locals in Gettysburg, I remember being shown, at least twice, their childhood collections of Mason jars filled with bullets—the famous minié balls fired by most of the small arms used in the Battle of Gettysburg in 1863. Curiously, next to the jar of relatively modern projectiles was another jar, this one filled to the brim with arrowheads, also found in their youthful romps through the once blood-soaked fields. However, back then, I never put two and two together: that apparently as many arrows had once been launched as bullets, far more than could have been expended by mere hunting.

Maps show a demarcation line between Native American tribes very near where Gettysburg now lies. Even more intriguing is that, down through the ages, echoes a mysterious name for a great pre-historic battle that took place in the area. Nineteenth Century native of the area, Emmanuel

Bushman heard it called "The Battle of the Crows," and wrote about it twice, intimating a lingering ghostly presence in the area of Native American spirits.

The National Park Service historians, whose interest in the history of Gettysburg extends tangentially beyond the three tumultuous days in July 1863, are also aware that some big Native American battle may have taken place in the area. I remember, while doing some research at the park library, talking to the chief historian at the time. She was excited because an aerial survey being conducted on the park seemed to reveal a huge Native American burial mound. Later I asked about it and was told that they were mistaken, that a field survey revealed nothing. I always wonder though—because of my own experiences at the park—whether that was the truth, or "disinformation" aimed at keeping curious visitors from exploring and possibly destroying a delicate, perhaps unprotectable area.

Keeping in mind the legends of the Native American battle, I received a letter from a woman living not too far from the battlefield of Gettysburg. She had been a reenactor and so was familiar with the area having visited numerous times.

Her interest in the paranormal aspect of Gettysburg had been piqued by photographs she took containing "mysterious gray spheres." She wrote that they had experienced some interesting happenings in visits to the Triangular Field...but not associated with the Civil War.

Her experiences in the oddly shaped field once sodden with the blood of Americans had to do with the earliest Americans to occupy and apparently fight over those fields.

In her letter she did not say that she had read about the rumors of the Native American battle there. Instead she simply states with certainty that "there were other battles fought there long before the North and South clashed upon this piece of ground."

In fact, her next paragraph states how she and her husband often "felt the presence of the Old Ones there." Their daughter seemed to attract the child spirits and would run along with them through the field.

The writer and her husband (their daughter was not with them) had walked to the bottom of the Triangular Field and got split up because of the underbrush. They both suddenly froze. She heard herself say, "Oh my God—this is where they herded them when they killed them!" Her husband also felt and psychically "saw" the same vision. They were transported into the past several hundred years and witnessed an attack upon a small village. She suddenly recalled trying to assist mothers and their children to flee through a wooded area. Her husband's vision was of himself shooting arrows from a bow at their attackers then being struck in the chest by a projectile.

The vision lasted about two or three minutes. When it was over, they could feel their hearts pounding in their chests. The simultaneous, similar psychic experiences suggest that they both had passed through a temporary portal or "warp" in time, dropping into a scene from the past. A couple years later, their daughter had a similar experience.

She had walked off the worn path about three-quarters of the way down the field. Suddenly she stopped and began shaking and crying. For the moment she was paralyzed. She began mumbling, "I died here—my child was killed running to me and died in my outstretched arms. And then I died here, too."

The writer expressed the opinion that the massacre that occurred there was brutal and complete, and that for such a small plot of earth the area, which would become the Triangular Field, has seen more than its share of death. In a final, spiritual plea she added, "May we always be aware we do not walk this world alone."

LITTLE ROUND TOP

...thy soul's flight,
If it find heaven, must find it out tonight.

—William Shakespeare, *Macbeth*

Little Round Top. With the diminutive in the name, the hill on the southern end of the battlefield of Gettysburg would lead the uninitiated student of the battle to think it wasn't very important. Though it rises 150 feet above the valley floor through which Plum Run meanders to the west of it, Little Round Top is 130 feet below its larger counterpart to the south, Big Round Top.

Little Round Top

But to the soldiers who fought upon the hill, it was not diminutive, not in their immediate experience there, nor for the rest of their lives, in their haunting memories and fear-filled, recurrent nightmares.

They never called it Little Round Top. In fact, they may never have known a name for it. In after action reports it was referred to by many names: Broad Top, Granite Spur (of Round Top), and Sugar Loaf being just a few from the Official Records. But for several reasons, the smaller geological brother of the large hill to the south became superior tactically.

The owners of the land, the Weikert family, had cut firewood and cleared the west side of the hill during the autumn before the battle. So the smaller of the round tops had a clear field of fire to the west, but the larger one was still forested. Confederates, in Longstreet's broad sweep toward the Union army's left flank, after driving in Sickles's advanced line, actually crested Big Round Top. The climb up the south slope in the summer heat and without water (canteens were sent to the rear and the advance started before the bearers returned) was more costly than Yankee bullets at that point. The southerners virtually collapsed at the summit to rest and catch their breath.

It is a maxim of war that the high ground is vital to tactical success, which is why even in modern warfare when hills do not have names, their numbers, usually referring to their height marked on maps, become associated with death and destruction. The maxim of seizing the high ground is why there is some discussion about why Big Round Top was not utilized by the Confederates when they were there on the afternoon of July 2, to dominate even Little Round Top.

Looking around, Confederate officers realized that, in the thick nearly impenetrable woods on the summit of Big Round Top, it was impossible to locate the enemy.

At least one historian suggested that a few dozen axes in the hands of the Alabamians who stopped on the crest of Big Round Top and an hour's hard work would have cleared the summit and allowed Confederate artillery to enfilade the entire Union position. I think it may have been a little more difficult than that.

First, the Confederates desperately needed a rest just to continue their march downhill to strike the Union line forming below them. Second, since in some places the southern slope of Big Round Top is almost sheer rock cliffs, an alternate, circuitous route—perhaps even a road—would have to be found and cut to bring artillery to the top. Third, orders were orders, and the Confederate officers would have had to send couriers back to alert their superiors of what they had found, superior officers would have to reconnoiter, sappers (engineers) would have to be consulted, equipment would have to be found to cut and move the trees, and so forth. Finally, they really had no time to waste. While in the dense woods on Big Round Top, the Confederates really couldn't find the enemy visually.

But within minutes of their arrival at the summit, their enemy found them.

A story that some dispute is that Maj. Gen. G. K. Warren, of the engineers, was on Little Round Top, with its magnificent view shed, watching Longstreet's men drive Sickles's troops back toward the Union line. Something caught his eye to the south in the woods of the big hill above him. He ordered an artillery piece to lob a shell into the woods. Confederate soldiers reflexively ducked to avoid the shell and falling broken limbs from the trees. Sunlight glittered from their burnished arms in a long, sparkling line on Big Round Top and Warren knew there were soldiers hidden in the woods—and they didn't belong to his army. He sent a rider to commandeer the first troops he found and bring them to the little, barren hill.

The courier ran into Col. Strong Vincent and told him of Warren's order. Looking about, the importance of Little Round Top was suddenly obvious. Sensing impending catastrophe Vincent ordered his men to the hill and rode ahead to find tactically sound positions. Lt. Col. Joshua Chamberlain and the men of his 20th Maine Regiment drew the short straw and were placed at the very end of the Union line and told to hold the position at all costs.

The rest is military legend: His line bent back practically upon itself by numerous assaults from the Confederates who had just vacated Big Round Top, his men calling for ammunition as they ran out, casualties depleting his unit's strength by the minute, Chamberlain ordered "bayonet!" and a maneuver resembling a swinging gate, bringing the bent-back (or "refused") companies in line with the others. Simultaneously, Lt. Holman Melcher ordered the rest of the 20th Maine to charge down the hill into the 15th Alabama Regiment of Confederates just as they were climbing the hill to attack the Maine men. Severe fighting rolled down the southern and eastern slopes and into the saddle between the Round Tops. An isolated company of the 20th Maine ended up attacking the Alabamians from the rear, increasing their disposition to withdraw. Chamberlain managed to hold his position by temporarily evacuating it. Three decades later he would receive the Congressional Medal of Honor for his role.

But the battle for the hill continued. Confederates renewed their attack along the western slope. Col. Strong Vincent, a Pennsylvanian defending his native state, was mortally wounded leading his brigade on Little Round Top. Brig. Gen. Stephen H. Weed was also mortally wounded atop the hill. Lt. Charles E. Hazlett, a veteran of some eight previous battles, whose artillery battery had been placed upon the hill, was summoned by Weed. Fate chose Weed to act as the Grim Reaper this day: Hazlett leaned over Weed to hear some final commands and was shot, falling across Weed's body. Irish immigrant Patrick O'Rorke, now a colonel in the Union Army, had been ordered by Warren himself to the hill. He and the men of his regiment, the 140th New York Infantry, barely had time to catch their breaths as they crested the hill and plunged down the other side into advancing Confederates. O'Rorke stood upon a rock to guide his troops and paid for his conspicuousness with his life, shot through the neck. According to historian Garry Adelman in his book *Little Round Top: A Detailed Tour Guide*, of 2,996 Union troops engaged at Little Round Top, 565 became casualties, which includes 134 killed, 402 wounded and 29 missing. The Southern cost for their futile attempts at taking the hill? Out of some 4,864 engaged there were 1,185 casualties, with 279 killed, 868 wounded and 219 missing.

The reason for the high cost in officers and men? Little Round Top, or Sugar Loaf, or Granite Spur, was considered by those who were in a position to decide, the key to the battlefield for the Union Army. The only problem is, most of that recognition came a couple of decades after the war.

One who did recognize its immediate importance was Maj. Gen. Gouverneur K. Warren, whose much photographed statue is placed upon the rock where he supposedly stood to observe the fighting of Maj. Gen. Sickles' Third Corps stretched from Devil's Den, through the Wheatfield to the Peach Orchard.

Some modern historians, however, feel that Warren's concern was misplaced; that Little Round Top was not as important as he imagined.

Military instinct told nearly everyone—from privates to major generals—that the bald hill commanded that part of the battlefield. From the valley it appeared that artillery would be able to enfilade—fire the length of—the entire Union line from Little Round Top to the cemetery, so it was important for the Federals to deny it to their enemy. But once they arrived at the summit with their big guns, Union artillerists realized that there was only a narrow ridge on top upon which to line up their cannon, and they could only face west. If Confederates had gained the summit and had managed somehow to drag their cannons and caissons from Seminary Ridge, across the valley, through the woods and across the farm fields, up the slope through the Triangular Field or through the rocky Plum

Run gorge and up the face of Little Round Top, only one or perhaps two guns would have been able to line up to rake the Union line from the flank.

Perhaps the one advantage to taking Little Round Top for the Confederates was that they were that much closer to seizing the road south to Taneytown, just a couple hundred yards to the east. They had already captured the Emmitsburg Road when they established their battle line along Seminary Ridge. In other words, from Little Round Top, they were in position to capture the second of three routes of retreat for the Union Army should the Federals need them.

In addition, several hundred yards beyond the Taneytown Road to the east, was the Baltimore Pike. After capturing Little Round Top the Confederates would have potentially been in between the Union Army and their capital in Washington.

But this too is mere speculation. There was a lot going on behind Little Round Top where units of the Union Army Sixth Corps and others were being held in reserve within striking distance of the Taneytown Road. All in all, had they conquered the lowest of the two hills, Confederates may not have been able to do much with it.

A number of years ago I returned to my roots and presented a talk on the ghosts of Gettysburg to the Western Reserve Civil War Round Table in northern Ohio. There I met a local school teacher who told me a story about a sighting by numerous witnesses on Little Round Top that seemed to defy any normal explanation, but perhaps confirm a paranormal one.

He confided in me that he and his fellow teacher were pretty much skeptics—his friend even more than he—when it came to ghosts. Annually the two of them accompanied a group of eighth grade middle school students from Ohio to Washington, D.C. with an afternoon stopover in Gettysburg. They would visit the National Cemetery, the now defunct electric map museum, and take a battlefield tour with a licensed battlefield guide. This particular year the two teachers decided to ride on different buses.

It was mid-March when the trip occurred. By the time the first busload of students reached Little Round Top, it was nearing dusk, but some of the students pointed out to the teacher that there was a soldier standing in the doorway of the famous "castle" monument to the 44th New York perfectly silhouetted by the light from the setting sun. According to the teacher he could see that the figure did indeed resemble a soldier with his military "tunic," officer's slouch hat, and what may have been a sword at his side. He assured the students that the figure could be nothing more than a reenactor and that they should try to meet him and ask some questions about his uniform and the battle. He related that most reenactors are well versed in the minutia of the common soldiers' lives and they certainly would get a wealth of knowledge from him. With the energy and enthusiasm only eighth graders can muster, they swarmed out of the bus and ran up to the monument. Their teacher followed a little more slowly.

Halfway to the monument he was met by some of the students. In spite of the fact that they rushed to the monument within seconds of seeing the "reenactor," they couldn't find him anywhere. Like good cavalry scouts, the kids had fanned out along the open crest of the storied hill but to no avail. One had even climbed up the stairs to the top of the castle to see if he'd gone up. He hadn't. But even from that high vantage point, the officer was nowhere to be seen.

After searching for several minutes, the teacher and his students moved toward their guide who was presenting the story of the fight for Little Round Top at General Warren's statue. When he was done, the teacher asked if he knew where the reenactor had gone. He was met with a frown and given the information that reenactors were rare if not non-existent on the battlefield in mid-March. They normally appeared from late spring to late summer, and again during Remembrance Day weekend in mid-November.

44th New York Monument

The teacher explained what he and the students had just experienced: seeing the soldier in the monument, then, just half a minute later, finding no trace whatsoever of him. As there were students going up the few pathways from the parking lot and reaching the site where he had been seen in record time, there was no way he could have gotten off the hill without being seen.

Licensed Battlefield Guides are a no-nonsense group of professionals who stick to what can be documented about the battle. But like everyone else who spends much time on the battlefield, they too are periodically confronted with the inexplicable. This particular guide had apparently heard the stories from others. He smiled at his confused group of students and their skeptical teacher and explained that a lot of people had seen that soldier and wanted to speak with him, but no one he knew had ever succeeded in doing so. The teacher asked him, was it possible that they had all seen a ghost in the dusk that evening? The guide simply replied that he wasn't supposed to talk about things that weren't battle-related, and continued his talk about the battle for the hill that had created so many ghosts.

Going through my files I found a letter from a young lady in her teens. It was August and she was visiting Little Round Top to watch the sunset with her father and cousins. It was a rare instance when they were the only ones on the hill, especially during the sunset display that is legendary. Sitting on a rock near the Warren statue, she and her cousin were quiet, contemplating, perhaps, the ironic contradiction of a place so beautiful that once filled the senses with all the horror and fear only combat can supply.

Although it was a summer evening, after a few minutes sitting she wrote that the hair on her arms and the back of her neck stood up. As she gazed down the hill into the gathering darkness, she noticed a blue mist materializing. It may have been more of a light she saw rather than a mist, because she wrote, "I say mist for lack of a better word. If you could see someone's aura, I think that is what it would look like."

As she peered into the blue mist she could make out the figure of a young man. The boy stood stiffly as if at attention. She got the impression from his youthful appearance that he may have been a drummer-boy, though she didn't see a drum. He stood just eight feet from her.

She said she was afraid to move, of scaring him off. But just as quickly as he had appeared, he vanished back into the world from where he had come.

She sat, not saying anything to her cousin because she thought she was the only one who had seen the apparition. But a few moments later her cousin turned to her with a stunned look on her face and said, "Did you see it?"

They shared what each had seen. The accounts differed only in the fact that her cousin was positive that she had seen a drum. Her main concern was not that she and her cousin had seen the same ghostly apparition appear then disappear before their eyes, but that a young man was thrown into the horror of battle as a drummer-boy.

Usually, when the actual fighting began, the drummer-boys would be sent to the rear. Yet they were not sheltered from the horror. They became stretcher-bearers and surgeons' assistants, witnessing the grim aftermath of the battle. And, though "civilized" warfare forbade the shooting of children, some were wounded and some killed by a stray bullet or shell.

It is almost impossible to keep up with all the letters and photos I receive from people relating their stories about unexplainable experiences in and around Gettysburg. Since the very first *Ghosts of Gettysburg* volume, I have gotten hundreds of letters, many of which begin, "I've never had a paranormal experience in my life…then we came to Gettysburg and…."

I received an email from a man who had visited Gettysburg and took a photograph from the top of Devil's Den toward Little Round Top. He had visited our *Ghosts of Gettysburg* headquarters and presented it to the individual at the desk who suggested he email it directly to me. In it he gave details as to when he had taken the photo he entitled "Gettysburg Soldier." He took the photo some four years before and apparently had analyzed it numerous times and enlarged it to do so, guaranteeing he had not changed or enhanced it. In fact he frankly asked if what he interpreted as a soldier could be a terrain feature.

I knew there was a statue in the famous "Valley of Death" and so I withheld my opinion until I had a chance to visit the site. Looking at the statue I realized that it was facing the wrong way—toward Hauck's Ridge and not Little Round Top as the figure in the photo, and the wrong color—white stone while the photo image was dark.

As well, the photographed soldier appeared translucent.

I emailed the photographer for more information and he too was perplexed when he first saw it. He hadn't taken two of the same shot—something paranormal investigators usually do, since apparitions often move in and out of the visual spectrum quickly. (The theory is that those from the other dimension cross frequencies in the electromagnetic spectrum and so are in the visible frequency spectrum only briefly.) So I went out to the exact spot where the picture was taken and discovered that there was nothing appearing in the field that could have been mistaken for what appeared in the photo.

My first thought was that it might have been a lone scrub pine near the flat rock, but the shape is wrong if compared with other scrub pines on the side of the hill. It is even more obvious that this image is in the shape of a human rather than a tree when the photo is enlarged.

And even more so in the enlargement, you can see completely through his legs to the rock behind him. Could this be the soldier seen by the school students just a few years before?

And finally, I received a letter and photo from a woman who was visiting Gettysburg with her younger brother. Included in the tour was a stop at Little Round Top. She took out her 35mm camera and took a shot of the Warren statue to include with the rest of her photos of the day. They returned home and enjoyed the memories from the photos when they were developed.

A couple of weeks after, her brother wanted to see the Gettysburg photos again. As she was shuffling through the prints she suddenly stopped and called her brother's attention to one photo in particular, the one they had taken on Little Round Top. In the background was the intended subject of the photo, Gen. G. K. Warren. But in the foreground was an image that had not appeared when they first looked at the picture. Now in the photo was a dark, shadowy figure appearing to have its head bowed. The shape of the head seems to indicate that the figure is wearing a kepi-style, Civil War era cap.

The photo is also dark; all the others on the roll turned out clear and bright. At first she thought it might have been a double exposure, but she never had a problem with a double exposure before. In fact, with most modern 35mm cameras I owned it was virtually impossible to take an accidental double exposure because of the film advancing systems.

She ruled out a double exposure from camera movement of the background Warren subject because the image is so different: appearing hunched over, different size, different style hat and not holding the binoculars present in the Warren statue's hand.

However, there is the paranormal phenomenon of "shadow people." Although most people think that all ghosts are white, like Casper, there are dark entities that have appeared throughout history and have been seen on the Gettysburg Battlefield. Could she have captured one on film?

Other than being confused as to why the image did not "develop" until a couple of weeks after the rest of the picture had been developed, the only other thing she mentioned was that it gave her the chills to think that they may have been that close to a soldier from another century and perhaps, another plane of existence.

DÉJÀ VU

*...He not busy being born
Is busy dying.*

—Bob Dylan

After collecting ghost stories about Gettysburg for close to fifty years, and publishing them for nearly half that time, some unique and informative data has emerged. Perhaps the most important (for paranormal studies), as well as intriguing fact is that many of the paranormal events I recorded decades ago have re-occurred.

This is more than just an interesting fact. It may be one of the proofs for paranormal activity: That the same events happen in the same place to multiple sets of people at different times. In fact, that is just how I became interested in recording the supernatural events at Gettysburg early in my career.

As well, it speaks to some of the more intellectual studies of the paranormal from iconic figures in the past. It may be another link in the chain of proofs we all seek to confirm: that there is indeed a personal existence after death; that death is not a door that is closing, but one that is opening.

Historically speaking, this phenomenon of repeating paranormal events leads us to the famous psychologist Carl Jung's theory of synchronicity. It states that events are "meaningful coincidences" if they occur with no causal relationship yet seem to be meaningfully related.

But Jung's concept was more sophisticated and more scientific. In fact, he used it to help explain the paranormal.

Jung invented the word "synchronicity" to describe "temporally coincident occurrences of acausal events." In other words, similar events that share no single cause. In one of his books he wrote: "How are we to recognize acausal combinations of events, since it is obviously impossible to examine all chance happenings for their causality? The answer to this is that acausal events may be expected most readily where, on closer reflection, a causal connection appears to be inconceivable."

In his book, *Jung on Synchronicity and the Paranormal*, Roderick Main wrote:

> The culmination of Jung's lifelong engagement with the paranormal is his theory of synchronicity, the view that the structure of reality includes a principle of acausal connection, which manifests itself most conspicuously in the form of meaningful coincidences. Difficult, flawed, prone to misrepresentation, this theory none the less remains one of the most suggestive attempts yet made to bring the paranormal within the bounds of intelligibility. It has been found relevant by psychotherapists, parapsychologists, researchers of spiritual experience and a growing number of non-specialists. Indeed, Jung's writings in this area form an excellent general introduction to the whole field of the paranormal.

Jung, it would appear, was transfixed by the idea that life was not a series of random events, but rather an expression of a deeper order.

One of the more interesting coincidences about the battlefield of Gettysburg is that it may have been a battlefield before the famous 19th Century battle. Centuries before.

I wrote about the legendary Native American battle in earlier *Ghosts of Gettysburg* volumes, in *Cursed in Pennsylvania*, as well as, in an earlier chapter in this book.

Recently, on a quest for other information for this book, I re-opened the pages of *A Strange and Blighted Land, Gettysburg: The Aftermath of a Battle*, by Gregory A. Coco. Anyone who knew Greg was astounded by his ability to find the most amazing forgotten facts about the battle in the archives. In one chapter he wrote about the area of the battlefield around the famous "Copse of Trees" and the legendary "Angle" of the stone wall. He mentioned that during a visit in May 1878, by President Rutherford B. Hayes, one attending correspondent, for some reason (perhaps because he heard it mentioned by a local historian during the visit), wrote that the "Angle" where the stone wall goes from north/south to east/west orientation and then back to north/south was "the geometrical centre of the occupied land" of the Susquehannock Indian Nation. He mentioned to his editor in Philadelphia the presence at the "Angle" of a one hundred ton boulder bearing the carved image of a tomahawk. While he was there, a grizzled Union veteran of Hancock's Corps (which defended the area from Pickett's Charge) was looking at the sign and mumbling to himself, "It's so, it's so; they foresaw the great battle, a curse to the white man, to boys in blue and gray."

The soldier was now destitute, a tramp, and had travelled many miles to see the carving once again and ponder its deeper meaning. He often wondered whether this mark did not cause the great battle. Perhaps he also wondered, as I have opined in *Cursed in Pennsylvania* whether Gettysburg had once been cursed to be a battlefield a second time, centuries after the great Native American "Battle of the Crows." The correspondent ended his missive with an observation: "Superstition was everywhere [as I glanced] from the man of brown rags to the purple and yellow spotted butterfly...balancing above the protruding end of a human bone."

So the synchronicity question remains: was Gettysburg fore-ordained to be a killing ground, christened first by the massive effusion of blood drawn, not by soft lead minié balls but by razor-sharp wedges of flint and marked by the carving on a strategically located boulder of a Native American weapon?

THE TEXAN

One of the first ghost stories I ever heard as a park ranger was told by a young woman who had a firsthand experience that I documented in *Ghosts of Gettysburg*. As rangers at the information desk, we got enough enquiries about ghosts at Gettysburg that we finally asked our supervisors what we should tell people. "Tell them there are no such things as ghosts and there are no ghosts here at Gettysburg." After having personally collected well over a thousand stories (scores still unpublished) and filling eight volumes with stories of the ghosts of Gettysburg, I now realize we were inadvertently misleading the visitors. (As well, when we were asked so many times by visitors if they had gotten all the bodies once buried on the battlefield, we inquired of those same supervisors what we should tell them. "Tell them, yes." As recently as 1996, however, remains of a soldier were found near the Railroad Cut. No doubt more still lie on the field to be discovered someday.)

Nevertheless, the young lady proceeded to tell us how she had stopped at Devil's Den early that morning, got out of her car and climbed to the top of a rock to take a photo and, despite the fact that there were no other cars in the remote area, she had the distinct feeling she was not alone. Turning, she saw behind her a man she described as a "hippie," disheveled, long hair, floppy hat, ragged clothes, barefoot. He spoke to her and said, "What you're looking for is over there," and pointed past her. She turned to look but, realizing that this stranger couldn't possibly have known what she was looking for, turned immediately back to find that, with nowhere to hide in the open area atop the boulders, he had vanished into thin air.

Incredibly, the ragged soldier she saw fit the description of the Texas troops at Gettysburg, whose early-war uniforms had been pretty much used up after two years in the field. Procuring new uniforms from far-away Texas was a task, so the Texans "borrowed" hats from farmers on the march, "liberated" shirts from hanging laundry, and "stole" pants from dead Yankees. They were indeed a hodge-podge of uniforms. And it was Texans who wrested the area of Devil's Den from the Union soldiers in vicious, dangerous, "hide and seek" fighting around the huge boulders.

This story remains a fine example of the rare "intelligent," or "interactive" haunting where the spirit acknowledges and even speaks to the living percipient.

Within the last three years, two other interesting sightings at Devil's Den have occurred making this less a confusing singular ghost story than an example of an apparent pattern of haunting at Devil's Den.

I was at an autographing session at a local bookstore when a woman approached and told me she had a ghost story from Gettysburg. She began by telling me that she had been visiting Devil's Den. She was in a bit of a reverie while standing there, she said, at one point looking at the ground and admiring the beautiful blue flowers growing at her feet. Suddenly she felt a presence. She looked up and standing before her was a man dressed in very ragged clothes....

I stopped her right there. "Did you read my first book?" I asked, thinking she was recounting my original story to me.

"No," she said. "I haven't read any of your books."

Intrigued now, I asked her to continue.

"He was only about three feet from me. I don't know how he got so close without me seeing or hearing him. Like I said, he was barefoot, with ragged pants, shoulder-length hair and a big floppy hat. He pointed at my sweatshirt and said, 'First Texas.' I looked at where he was pointing and realized I was wearing my University of Texas sweatshirt. I looked up and that quickly he was gone."

Did she see the same soldier spirit who was seen by the first woman almost thirty years before? Does this Texan still remain in the jumble of rocks a century and a half after he fought—and perhaps died— to pry Devil's Den—a place whose name he probably never knew—from his mortal enemy, the Yankees?

Perhaps the answer lies in a second encounter I had as I was preparing this book. Autographing at a fundraiser for the Wounded Warriors Project, I met a man from New Jersey. He told me a story about how, after attending a football camp at Penn State, he and his father visited the Gettysburg Battlefield and ended up at Devil's Den.

> While there, I went up to the top of the rocks and my father was down below taking pictures of the surrounding area and of Little Round Top. While I was on the rocks I noticed a reenactor that was there (or what I thought was a reenactor). His look was very disheveled like he had been in battle, wearing a white shirt and black pants. I really didn't think anything of it being it was the weekend of the reenactment, so I turned and was looking around and that's when I noticed that the parking lot was empty below except for our car and nobody was parked by the Triangular Field.... Now I had heard the stories of the spirits at Devil's Den, but at that time I didn't believe in ghosts.

He describes pretty much the same, open, panoramic view as the woman in the story from some thirty years before. Looking back, to his amazement, he realized that the "disheveled" figure had disappeared.

> At that point, after trying to debunk the sighting (which I couldn't find a logical reason why he disappeared), I realized I must have seen a ghost. Since then every time I've been in Gettysburg at Devil's Den I always ask him to show himself. This experience is how I got interested in the paranormal and became a paranormal investigator. I wished I could have tried to communicate with him and ask him why he is still

there and what his message is that he is trying to send to people.

THE RECURRING SIGHTINGS OF GENERAL REYNOLDS

Of all the ghost stories of Gettysburg that I've collected, there is only one that can be definitively connected to an individual who died at Gettysburg, and who reappears fairly frequently.

The Lutheran Theological Seminary at Gettysburg was established in 1826 in a building on the corner of Washington and West High Street. By 1832, the Seminary had outgrown its humble beginnings and moved to the ridge to the west of the town of Gettysburg between the road to Fairfield and the road to Cashtown. Soon the ridge was being called Seminary Ridge. During the Battle of Gettysburg, it became the main Confederate battle line and would associate its name with others like Devil's Den, Little Round Top and Cemetery Ridge written in American History in human blood.

Linked to the battle as temporary hospitals, I've written about some of the buildings at the Seminary in previous volumes. Stories have been reported from a residence building of explosive poltergeist activity attributed to one soldier who had been buried and trapped under a pile of decomposing corpses in the cellar. When he was found days after the battle, he was raving and died in that condition a few days later. His is the perturbed spirit that caused the residents to call in a priest to cleanse the house and cellar.

Some of the first stories I'd heard about Krauth House, another residence building sitting prominently on the north end of Seminary Ridge, told of strange noises, like books being thrown around, emanating from the attic where, coincidentally, blood-stained books had been found. Some speculated they had been used as makeshift pillows for shattered heads and torn limbs of young men wounded in the battle. Another story from Krauth House centered on a closet. Told to keep the door closed when he slept, one young seminarian forgot, and in the middle of the night, to his regret, found out why he had been told that odd piece of information....

Krauth House

A woman who had attended the Seminary in the 1980s had written to me after reading the first two volumes of the *Ghosts of Gettysburg* series. She said the experiences she had while living in Krauth House could only be described as "otherworldly."

She had lived in Krauth House on three different occasions. The first time she lived on the second floor near the stairs to the attic. One night she had skipped dinner to work on a paper. While concentrating, she heard some strange sounds coming from the attic: the shuffling of feet and whistling. At first she ignored it and it stopped. Then it started up again, only louder. She rose from her work and went out her door to be confronted by another student who had heard the sounds as well. After affirming that the weird sounds came from neither of them, that fact was proven by the shuffling and whistling beginning again. They were sure there was no one in the house but them. They realized that if anyone was to find out who was making the noise, it had to be them.

They "marched loudly" up the stairs to the attic to scare off whomever, or as she wrote, "whatever" it was. They turned on the light and found not a soul in either room of the attic. Her friend said a prayer for whomever—or whoever's soul—it was that remained in the attic. The woman said that during the rest of the year, from time to time, she would again hear the shuffling and whistling of the wandering invisible entity.

Her second stay in Krauth was more frightening. Sometime during the night, generally around 3:00 A.M., she would wake up with the feeling that someone was pressing her down on the bed. She wrote that it was the distinct feeling of hands holding down her ankles and shoulders. Like many who have experienced "sleep paralysis" or, as it is known in some paranormal circles, "Old Hag Syndrome," she wrote it off to weird dreams.

Then, after a late night discussion at one of the local 24-hour diners, she realized that she was not the only Seminarian experiencing the horrifying feeling of being man-handled out of sleep. Several of the women present and some of the men who lived in other dormitories had been subjected to the same experience. Someone attempted to explain it—and they all agreed—that they might be having the same feeling that a wounded soldier would have when surgeons would have orderlies physically hold them down, so they could do their hideous work without the patient struggling.

One of the housemates in Krauth confided that she had rid herself of the abusive intruder by calling upon the name of the Father, Son, and Holy Spirit, and commanding whatever it was to release her. It worked.

Finally, she related that her last year at the Seminary she lived on the first floor near the front door and the door into the cellar. She said there was a closet in that room that made her "very, very uncomfortable." There were actually two closets in the room, but just the one had an effect on her. Despite the radiator being too hot to touch, the room would periodically be plunged into an icy cold. And she would be awakened some nights by someone loudly descending the cellar steps. One night it angered her that someone would be doing laundry in the middle of the night, so she opened the cellar door to yell at them. She was shocked to see that there were no lights on in the cellar and no one there.

Baughman Hall

Baughman Hall on the Seminary campus was built in the 1950s and sits closest to the Fairfield Road. Some rumors have it being built on the scene of a "storage area" for the dead of the battle; others relate that when it was being built, human bones were unearthed during the digging for the foundation.

One room on the third floor seems to be the most active. A former resident remembers strange metallic noises coming from somewhere in the room. One night while the occupant was asleep, his locked door flew open. Startled awake, he was even more surprised to realize that the bolt on the open door was still in the locked position. It affected the student so profoundly that he ran from the room to sleep elsewhere that night.

Upon occasion, the radio in the room would turn itself on. Inspection assured the occupant that there were no loose wires or short circuits in the device to make it begin to play on its own. As well, the hallmark of a haunting would periodically occur in that particular room: almost instantly the air would turn freezing cold inside the room.

Another later occupant of that same room experienced the terrifying phenomenon of sleep paralysis. He was apparently sleeping on his stomach. In the middle of the night he awoke and attempted to rise, but it felt like a physical being was pressing down on his back not allowing him to move.

So why would a place of solemn prayer and godliness be prone to haunting? Though some religions fervently deny the existence of ghosts, could there be more "spirit" in spirituality than they are willing to concede?

With the carnage, destruction, and death that swirled with great savagery around the once peaceful Lutheran Theological Seminary during the first tumultuous day of the Battle of Gettysburg, it is no wonder that strange, unexplainable, supernatural events happen there, even in the relatively modern buildings built long after the battle left such personal agony in its wake. But one individual seems to show up who was once identified by a seminarian.

The story associated with several sightings and odd, unexplained events in some of the newer buildings at the seminary seem to revolve around Maj. Gen. John F. Reynolds, who was shot and killed within sight of the older Seminary buildings.

The original story of his sighting (*Ghosts of Gettysburg II*) came from a Seminarian who lived in one of the newer buildings at the south end of the Seminary and was awakened in the middle of the night by a scream from down the hall. Relegating it to a dorm-mate reveling, he went back to sleep, only to awakened an hour later by a visible presence in his room: a darkly-bearded man dressed in a blue coat, leaning against his dresser looking at him. He shouted at it, prayed, and finally stood to confront the intruder, whereupon it vanished before his eyes. Later that week he ran into his dorm-mate whom he had heard scream that same night, who told him that he had seen the head of a dark-bearded soldier floating in his room. That is what made him scream.

Two visions of the same ghost within an hour, both of the same man who closely resembled the general who had died within shouting distance of their dormitory.

More recently I received a letter from a woman who had taken our Seminary Ridge Tour, which featured the ghost stories of the Seminary. They had gotten to the Schmucker House when the woman felt a cold chill surround her. She dropped back from the group and began taking pictures.

That evening, after she had fallen asleep, she began having strange, reoccurring dreams concerning the death of General Reynolds. In the dreams she was standing on the porch of the Schmucker House watching as Reynolds was struck by the fatal minié ball.

Then it got personal.

In the dream, as the general was falling from his horse, he reached out toward the woman and called for her to help him. But she was frozen; she couldn't move or talk and watched helplessly as he perished. She looked around and all she could see was bloodshed and death. If it had happened once, it could be explained. But the same dream crept into her sleep the next three nights.

She finally took the film to be developed. Every picture she took of the tour came out white. The only one that developed (although darkly) was of the porch of the Schmucker House, where she was standing in her dream, and even that photo had some strange, feathery white anomalies showing on the right corner. She analyzed it and confirmed there had been no people or things on that side of her to pollute the photo. She sent all the photos to me for confirmation.

Why, though, would some of the newer buildings on the Seminary campus hold the spirit of the general officer who had died some ninety years before they were even built?

From documents and testimony of Reynolds's aides, we know he was taken from where he was shot to a small stone cottage on the Emmitsburg Road. Looking at a map, we can see that the modern dorms are on the route where his aides would have transported General Reynolds's body.

Also germane to our topic of déjà vu, the house where Reynolds was taken is the scene of at least two similar supernatural events, one of which I wrote about in a previous ghost book, another which I received a letter about.

The George George House on Steinwehr Avenue, in recent years, has housed Servant's Olde Tyme Photos where, during the day, visitors may have their photos taken dressed in reproduction 19th Century clothing. It is also where Reynolds's corpse was taken just before being transported to his home in Lancaster for burial. One night, a couple walking by looked in the window and saw what they thought was a pair of wax figures: one of a Union officer lying on a cot, either asleep or dead; the other an animated figure in a chair, reading a book and lifting a handkerchief to her eyes. The next morning when they entered the building and asked where the wax figures were, they were met with confusion since the staff had placed no wax figure display on the floor overnight. When the couple mentioned a door in a wall that was currently covered with a permanent display, the staff was amazed. Indeed there was an unseen door hidden behind the display.

George George House

Fast forward.

I received an email from a man who had a childhood memory jogged back to life when he watched one of the *Ghosts of Gettysburg* programs on television.

Keep in mind that I heard the story above from a third source, the man whose parents were renting the George George House before it became a photo shop. He had gotten it from his parents who had heard it from their employees. They apparently had left out something that was vital to the credibility of the story.

There were more than two witnesses.

In his email, the man reminded me of an earlier email he had sent regarding an experience he and his father had around 1971, when he was about thirteen years old. He had become an avid Civil War buff by that age and begged his father to take him to Gettysburg. His father suggested July 2 of that year since it was the anniversary of what most historians believe was the bloodiest day of the battle. Coming from Cleveland, they drove the five hours overnight and arrived before dawn.

He recalled pestering his father about which houses were in Gettysburg at the time of the battle; he remembered seeing the majestic statue of Maj. Gen. Reynolds and Lee's Headquarters, but because it was still too dark to see the battlefield, his father suggested they have breakfast before touring the field.

He remembered running up to one of the houses in town and peering in a window. There he saw a bearded Civil War soldier on a bed, which was four to six inches too short for his stature, in the middle of the room. Looking closer, he noticed another figure in the room, a girl, seated near the corner between the head of the bed and the wall. She was reading a small red book. He recalled that she appeared a little older than he was and struck him as attractive. She was dressed in a white gown with a hat. He noticed a lock of light brown hair had escaped from the front of the hat. His father caught up to him and saw the same scene. This being his first trip to Gettysburg, he thought it must be a reenactment of the death scene of General Reynolds, and that the young girl was a student at the local college receiving some kind of academic credit for her participation.

Just at this time a couple was walking by. Their interest was piqued by the father and son looking in the window, so they stopped to observe the scene. He remembered that the man was older than the woman, perhaps a father or friend, and they all watched together. It was this couple who was portrayed in the TV program.

The young man, with the mind of a teenager, took detailed mental notes of the experience. He remembered that the room was sparsely decorated; that the "general" did a good job of playing dead, showing no motion of breathing; that his lips were swollen and purple beneath his beard; and that his hair had been matted down by a hat.

He watched as the girl began to move. She took a purple bookmark and placed it between the pages of the book, closed the book and placed it at the head of the bed. She stared straight ahead for a moment, took a lace handkerchief that she held in her left hand, and dabbed at a tear in her left eye. His first thought was, "How fake. Nobody wipes their eye like that." Then the girl stood and walked right toward the young man peering into the window. He jumped back, expecting her to admonish him for intruding. But in her own world (or perhaps out of this one) she acted like she didn't see anyone in the window and passed right by. She entered a small closet-sized room opposite of where the outside observers stood.

In the room he could see a shelf upon which sat a metal or porcelain pan. In it was what appeared to be bloody water. He saw her pick up a cloth, ball it up and dip it in the water, then walk back to the body of the general and gently dab his forehead with the dampened cloth. She took the cloth back, returned to her chair and resumed her reading.

The young man ran over to the other side of the house to a window that was behind the young woman. He could see the book from which she read and the title at the top of the page. He pronounced it out loud—P-Salms—to the amusement of the man and woman who corrected him. The four watched for a few more minutes, then drifted away when nothing more happened inside the house.

Later that day, the father and son went back to see the "reenactment" again, only to be laughed at by the two ladies inside and told they were obviously at the wrong place.

Perhaps the ladies changed their minds when the second couple came in to see the "reenactment" and described the door they had seen, now hidden by a permanent display.

The 2015 email I received from the man attempted to interpret his youthful experience.

He had returned to Gettysburg on July 2, 2013, the 150th Anniversary of the battle and specifically returned, before dawn, to the George George House, hoping to see the same scene he had when he was a youth.

But the ghosts of Gettysburg are indeed fickle. Anniversary or not, for whatever reason, they manifest by a whim or a law as yet not fully understood by us mere mortals. He had no sighting that morning of a lovely young woman in mourning for a general officer of the Union Army killed in the line of duty.

He returned later to the house, now the well-known photography studio. A couple was getting their picture taken. After they were finished, he stood between the camera and where the couple had posed—the exact spot where he had seen the tableau years before. The photographer struck up a conversation and politely listened to the man's story. He said he remembered the filming of the story in the house, but added that the event never happened.

At first he was confused; he knew what he had seen. He also knew that historians have verified Reynolds's body being taken to the George George House before being sent to Baltimore via Westminster, Maryland, then to Philadelphia to lie in state, then Lancaster, the general's home for burial. (The photographer apparently was referring to the woman being there since there is no record of anyone but Reynolds's aides accompanying the body.)

So upon returning to Cleveland, he began researching the postmortem experiences of John Reynolds's body.

He found the Reynolds Family Papers in local university libraries and online. From his research he learned that Catherine Hewitt, Reynolds's secret fiancée, asked Sergeant Charles Veil, Reynolds's aide, to visit her at the Sisters of Charity, in Emmitsburg, Maryland, just a few miles from where her betrothed was slain in battle. True to her promise to Reynolds, she had joined a convent after his death. She gave Veil a small package as a keepsake. When he unwrapped it, he discovered a handkerchief with the seal of the United States she had embroidered upon it. As my correspondent wrote, "I bet that handkerchief was white with lace trim."

His theory was that Catherine, after hearing of the battle, had followed the army to Gettysburg, only to find her fiancé had been killed earlier. She pleaded with his aides to be able to hold vigil over his body that first night, to which they relented. As for the body that left Gettysburg for Westminster and Baltimore that night—it was a ruse. The next morning, Reynolds's body would be removed after his "Dear Kate" was allowed to spend her vigil.

The handkerchief she (or her spirit) was seen using to dry her mourning tears, according to the paranormal theorist, was the very same one she would present to Veil a few months later in Emmitsburg.

Catherine "Kate" Hewitt would follow the body to Baltimore, (according to the theorist) thence Philadelphia and announce herself to Reynolds's surprised family as the general's secret fiancée. They warmly embraced her and allowed her a second night's vigil with her betrothed.

"If new evidence some day proves this to be true," he wrote in a post-script, "then it was fore-told by two ghosts of Gettysburg."

The "official" account, written by Reynolds's aide Charles H. Veil appears in his book, *Personal Recollections and Reminiscences of the Civil War* and in it he writes that the general's body was taken the night of July 1, (and not the next morning) from Gettysburg in a wooden box that once contained a coffin, since all the coffins in Gettysburg after that bloody first day were already spoken for. The interesting thing is that Reynolds was apparently too tall for the box (just as he was too tall for the bed the witness saw in the George George House) and his aides had to knock out the end of the box for the General to fit.

But in fairness it seems that Charles Veil—like many writers of personal memoirs from the war—had a tendency to "embellish" some aspects of his accounts. In the memoirs, he alone is the one to drag Reynolds's body and save it from the advancing Confederates. However, in a letter to David M. McConaughy, a Gettysburg lawyer and notable citizen, he wrote on April 7, 1864, that two others—Captains Mitchell and Baird—were also present. The two took the general's legs and

Veil picked Reynolds up under the arms and carried him from the woods back to the Seminary.

When he met Reynolds's family before the funeral, they were already under the impression that he was the one who saved their brother's body from falling into the hands of the enemy. They all—apparently including Kate Hewitt—later visited Gettysburg to see exactly where on the battlefield Reynolds had fallen and to get their photo taken at Devil's Den. One of Reynolds's sisters wrote to Lincoln and secured a promotion for Veil from Private to Second Lieutenant. His wartime and postwar military career was secured and he continued to correspond with the family.

He wrote his memoirs sometime in his mid-fifties. He unequivocally wrote that, "Not having any assistance, not one of our men being near, I picked him up by taking hold under his arms and commenced pulling him backward toward our line or the direction in which we had come from." To add to the drama, the Confederates were so close he could hear them commanding him to "drop him." He did write that, by the time he got Reynolds over the brow of the rise behind them, he found some men to help.

But Veil would not be the first autobiographer in history to forget some details from thirty-five years before or create some facts that bolstered a previous and important misconception, nor, I am certain, will he be the last.

The question is, do we believe him or a ghost scenario witnessed by four people?

THE HOUSE ON CARLISLE STREET

Still another example of paranormal synchronicity became apparent when, in the fall before the writing of this volume, I received a call from Shannon, a senior at Gettysburg College. It turned out that she had a minor in writing and actually used some of my *Ghosts of Gettysburg* books in a college project.

So my "team" of paranormal researchers for this preliminary investigation was small: my wife Carol and friend Mary

Duvall, who is sensitive to supernatural forces. I took along my recorder to document my interview and a few pieces of equipment: digital camera and gauss meter to detect any anomalous electromagnetic fields.

Passmore House

The house was built in 1895 by John C. Lower, born near Gettysburg in 1844 and a veteran of the Civil War, having served in the 21st Pennsylvania Cavalry. I had visited and wrote about the house before in *Ghosts of Gettysburg IV*. The woman who had co-owned the Queen Anne style "cottage" (an architectural term having nothing to do with the size of the 25-room house) had rented out the extra rooms to Gettysburg College women. Their experiences were typical of a haunted house in the northern part of town. Four of the housemates had heard someone moving around in the living room downstairs; cautious inspection revealed no living soul there. One Saturday in the fall, after returning from a football game, all of them noticed that their perfume bottles had been rearranged—moved—as if someone had been busy while they were gone cleaning up after them. It would happen again and again.

One night during the winter the women were in bed. They all heard footsteps roaming the hall. One by one they emerged from their rooms to realize it was not one of them who crept down the hall that night. One of the women heard them coming down the hall and stop at her open door. Slowly the door closed.

A séance produced the name "Joanna Craig," and the information that she had been a servant about 20 years of age. It was the impression of the women that it was she who sort of looked out for them: the microwave would turn on by itself, indicating to the women that someone was trying to cook for them; the TV channels would change without anyone touching the remote suggesting the proper programs to watch; and the women would often say that they had the feeling of someone watching over them.

(Interestingly, when the owner was excavating for a new porch, his shovel hit a stone. When he unearthed it, he realized it was a carved stone. To get it out of the way, he tossed it to one side. When he went to look at it later, across the top of the stone was carved the name, "Joanna Craig." The stone remains in the back yard where he threw it to this day.)

Whoever it was watching over the girls would scratch the pillowcase around a semi-sleeping woman's head. At least, that's what it sounded like to her: fingernails on her pillow. And when that happened, there were the whispers that came to her ears—but only when her eyes were closed—and stopped when she opened them to see who it was.

Finally, and perhaps most frighteningly, everyone in the house—including the owner—heard what they described as a body tumbling down the interior stairs and crashing to the first floor. They all ran to the staircase to find…nothing.

Virtually all of the activity in the house is classified as "poltergeist" activity—poltergeist meaning "noisy ghost"—consisting of physical objects being moved, doors slamming, lights being turned on and off, unexplainable noises, footsteps, motion and so forth.

My team and I interviewed Shannon and her housemates. We did an investigation and a cleansing of the one room that was the most active. We also attempted to gather EVP in the attic. The results were very interesting, especially in light of what we know about synchronicity.

I recorded the interviews with the current tenants. At the very beginning Shannon mentioned that she had awakened in the middle of the night and felt and heard something around her. She's had bouts with "sleep paralysis" before, otherwise known as "Old Hag Syndrome," the unnerving feeling of thinking you're awake but realizing that you cannot move. This event, however, wasn't a case of sleep paralysis. She could move, but still, when she opened her eyes whatever it was wasn't going away. She turned over and saw a woman's face looking down at her.

Somehow, she wasn't scared and felt instinctively that the woman wasn't evil. She grabbed her phone and turned on the flashlight app, and the woman vanished. That's when Shannon got scared. She looked at the clock and it was 4:00 A.M. She turned on a light in the room and slept the rest of the night with it on.

But as she lay there trying to get back to sleep, her window air conditioner began making a weird noise, something it had never done before. The strange noise continued, so she got up and turned the air conditioner off. She suddenly realized that, even with the air conditioner off, the room began to get cold. It was soon freezing in her room.

I asked how well she could see the woman, if she could pick up any details and she said yes. "Her hair was like this, straight back. I didn't see her body. She was like leaning over. I just saw her face. She was kind of smiling at me. She was trying to scare me. She was trying to mess with me. She was middle aged...."

About six in the morning she texted her housemates and two were awake. She told Nicole about it who said, "Okay, so I'm not crazy."

It seems that Nicole was having experiences in the house as well.

They apparently had some problems with locks on their doors. Shannon: "One of our first nights here our friend's door got locked, just like locked itself, and we had to break it down."

Nicole said, "That was my room right there," and pointed to a room just off the living room. "I would always out of habit close it [her door] and lock it constantly and every time...I'd check it and make sure I'd closed it and locked it and I'd come back and it would be unlocked and open. I'd be like, 'Why is this happening?' Every single time. But the door's broken and that's what I would blame it on. And then there was another time before I got the air conditioner that happened probably a week ago now. It was sweltering. One day I wake up and it's freezing, like I'm freezing, like my hair's standing up. I'm not scared at this point, I'm not afraid, just [thinking]'hmmm, that's bizarre.' It has not been cold in this room at all, ever."

Nicole continues relating her experience on the recorder. This time it involves a rare visual experience.

"So I was in my room looking for a shirt I needed for the day and I couldn't find it so I called Maddie [another housemate] and I hear her in there [the living room] and hear her moving. There's obviously a person in there. I was like, 'Oh, Mads, can I borrow a shirt, can I borrow this shirt? Maddie. Maddie. You can hear it [the person] the walls are so thin and I watch this person leave. I don't see the person, I just see the body, the arms and the bottom of them walk out of that room and I was like, there's undeniably a person in there. I go in, I look around, I didn't hear a door open or anything. But I watched them leave. That was another thing."

Nicole said that another housemate asked if anyone had heard the massive crash that woke her up. Shannon didn't remember hearing that particular crash, but remembered waking up at the time and finding that three other housemates were all awake. She walked down to Maddie's room and found that the freezing cold that she and Nicole had experienced in their room had now moved into Maddie's room.

Someone on the recorder, possibly Nicole, said, "It sounded like a big piece of furniture or something fell over." Those who heard it came downstairs and discovered nothing was disturbed.

Shannon asked me about my story of the house in *Ghosts of Gettysburg IV.* "You did mention that they [the previous tenants of the house, some 18 years before] had heard one time someone falling down the stairs?"

I couldn't recall the exact details of the story and I didn't know if they heard the tumbling of a body down the stairs. (Referencing the story later, I discovered the tenants and landlady did hear what sounded like a human body tumbling down the stairs.) All I said was, "They heard a big crash, something hitting the bottom of the stairs."

Nicole said that she didn't hear tumbling, yet another housemate said that she distinctly heard tumbling down the stairs.

Someone on the tape, probably Nicole, said "There was another one at 4:30 that I heard and I thought, someone fell, something broke. The second time was the one I heard and it was 4:30, because I remember looking at my clock and it wasn't the tumbling but just the end where I thought something dropped or something."

Shannon interjected, "Which is weird, because I heard this tumbling. When I woke up I saw them all texting and I was scared because I could just feel something. You just know when you wake up, like you can feel it. And I didn't want to open my eyes. I didn't want to see her again, because it was the same feeling. But then I heard my phone go off, I thought, ah people are awake."

Carol asked Nicole if she minded if she and Mary went back to her room. That room appeared to us to be a hot spot, perhaps even an energy vortex or, worse, a portal, and Carol and Mary wanted to find out. They left the interview to investigate.

Shannon tried to inject a little levity into the interview, which was now getting pretty intense for the women who had experienced it. "It kind of makes you a little crazy," she said, obviously about the house and their experiences in it. "But the other thing that happened with Maddie. We were just sitting here in the living room and we both look up to see that door, the closet door, just open. And we look at each other, and we just look down, like 'don't talk about it.'"

I looked over to the closet door. It was a heavy relatively ornate door typical to a house of the era.

One thing Shannon and Nicole mentioned was that the girls who lived in the house just the year before had had experiences as well.

I mentioned that one day I would like to interview them. They would make at least three sets of women who lived in that house that would have had experiences in the paranormal. I want to know how similar their experiences were.

Shannon: "And the girl that was in Nicole's room, she had the most of anyone."

Carol and Mary had returned from their investigation of Nicole's room. Often the mediums with which we work like to remain "under the radar," so to speak.

"I'm going to 'out' Mary right now," she said to the residents. "She's a sensitive. So what we found [in Nicole's room] was that she [the ghost] was trying to get help. She knew you could see her and that was exciting to her."

Shannon asked if she is the same one that's upstairs. Mary suggested that they might want to go upstairs and check.

Carol added, a little ominously, "Because we're thinking there's somebody else up there."

Shannon asked, "So do you think she knew I could see her when I turned around?"

"Oh yeah," Mary said. "They know."

Shannon seemed concerned and asked, "What does she want, though?"

Nicole too was worried and asked if she wanted to leave the house.

Carol said, "That's what we did." While she and Mary were in Nicole's room they helped the ghost "cross-over" to the other side, to move on. It's important to know, however, that once a ghost moves on to the other side, it is not necessarily permanent. They are still able to return, according to numerous mediums.

"There is so much heavy presence in there," Mary stated, "when we walked in, it felt like...." She stopped at the girls' expressions. "I know, you know."

The women begin talking over one another, but Carol reassures them that, as strange as the happenings in the house are, they are not out of the ordinary for a haunting and especially for that particular house which has been active for at least twenty years of my recording the events there. "No, you're not crazy," she said.

Carol, referring to the results of the investigation she and Mary had just conducted in Nicole's room, gave this bit of information. "Well, the ghost was from Chicago."

On the tape, there was a sudden intake of breath from all the tenants present. An unknown voice says, "Oh my God! That's where Paige's dad is from and she would always go to Chicago. She lives with her mom but...."

"Is there anyone else here?" Shannon asked.

"We still want to go up to your room," Carol said.

We went up to Shannon's room and she showed us the formerly noisy air conditioner whose effectiveness when it was off was enhanced by some supernatural phenomenon, and a jewelry holder that became the plaything of a poltergeist.

We also had an opportunity to go to the attic and see the spot at the attic window where the child of one of our guides, some fifteen years ago, had looked up and seen a woman standing by a hanging carpet appearing about to clean it with an old-fashioned rug beater. The child described her with her hair up in a bun, in an old-fashioned, high-necked dress with a brooch at her throat. That day, no one was at that window, and certainly no one dressed in 19th Century garb.

But I did attempt to gather some EVP (electronic voice phenomena) up in the over-heated attic. I made several attempts. I finally asked, "Joanna Craig, are you still taking care of these women?" referring, of course, to the spirit of the caring servant who still returns to make sure the ladies of the college are taken care of in her former employer's residence. Of course there was silence in the room even though the recorder indicated that something was being recorded. When I played it back, after my question about someone still taking care of the women in the house, a female voice was heard, answering, "Yes. I suppose I am."

After the attic, we descended all the way into the cellar. There I had an unexplainable, scientifically documented experience. My gauss meter—an instrument that picks up electromagnetic fields—was picking up a few stray hits, mostly where there was evidence of an electrical source. But when I got to the solid stone foundation wall just below Nicole's room—the most active room in the house—the gauss meter "pegged," with the needle hitting the maximum it could go. It was an "aha" moment for me. High EMF, besides possibly indicating the presence of a paranormal entity, can also *cause* hallucinations in the brain, which mimic paranormal events such as sightings and auditory events. Was this the cause of the mysterious hauntings in the room above?

But the more I examined, the more I realized, there were no electrical boxes or wires attached to or entering that wall. It was a solid stone wall, like the ones out on the battlefield, except about six feet high. Since the room above was actually built outward from this wall by enclosing a part of the porch, it was actually the foundation wall for the house. I must have studied that wall for fifteen minutes, until everyone had begun going upstairs, looking for any kind of electrical wires or devices leading into it, the whole time with the gauss meter wailing its warning for high-electromagnetic energy. I could find no evidence of anything going into or through that wall.

It was a solid stone wall.

THE BLUE BOY, THE TYPEWRITER LADY, & THE PARTY GHOST

Guides for the *Ghosts of Gettysburg Tours*, being among the public so much, are often recipients of ghost stories experienced by their customers. Devon, one of our veteran guides, provided updates for three haunted sites recorded in previous volumes.

One evening, two women on Devon's *Carlisle Street Tour* told her they attended Gettysburg College and lived in the room in Stevens Hall associated with the "Blue Boy." They had some experiences there.

The original story of the Blue Boy has been floating around the college for so long it has achieved legend status. It involved the hiding of a young boy—some say a runaway from the local orphanage—by some kind-hearted residents of the third floor of Stevens when it housed all-female students. The Homestead Orphanage operated under a foul-tempered matron in the last years before it was shut down, so the mid-1870s would be a likely date. One cold winter night the housemother of Stevens staged a surprise inspection and the students were forced to hide the runaway on the ledge outside the window while they were being questioned. When they returned, he had disappeared. And while his mortal form vanished, modern students see his face—now with a bluish tinge from the frigid cold he suffered—floating outside their window, three stories up.

The original sightings of the Blue Boy's face were decades ago, yet recurring images of the young man have been seen roaming the campus as recently as the past few years. Devon's customers' story adds to these mysterious tales.

Stevens Hall

They arrived at school earlier that year as freshmen. Their first Saturday night on campus came along and they left the room to attend one of the functions. When they came back, they discovered their window was open. Neither one of them had opened it.

With the first week of classes beginning, the incident was forgotten. Until the next weekend.

Again, on Saturday night, they went out, returned, and found the window flung open.

For the next few weeks, returning to their room was an anxious experience, always wondering if the window would somehow be open. But the activity seemed to subside, at least for the moment.

Thanksgiving vacation came and went, but when the roommates returned to campus they were called to the security offices. Security had to go to their room three times during the break to close the window, thinking the women had remained on campus or returned over the long weekend and forgot to close the window.

But the students protested their guilt: neither had returned over the break. They hadn't entered the room.

They finally asked some of the upper-class students what was going on. They were told they lived in the Blue Boy Room and finally heard the weird ghost story about it.

They got to thinking: if the entity was so active over just the long weekend, what would happen over the upcoming Christmas break when they would be gone for a month?

They decided to do a séance.

One night just before Christmas break, they sat in their room, determined to communicate with the tragic boy—or his spirit—who has now become famous on campus. They held hands and hummed and did their best to emulate what they thought happened during a séance. They finally addressed the Blue Boy telling him they didn't mind if he came into their room when they were absent. In fact, they invited him to come in any time they weren't there. "Just close the window," they told him. The next day, they left for Christmas break.

In a month they returned and met each other in the lobby. Climbing the stairs together, they opened the door and saw immediately that the window was closed. But there was another bigger problem.

The room was completely re-arranged. Their beds had been moved to different places, dressers were moved and personal items on their dressers had been moved around. Most bizarre was that the coffee maker was sitting in the middle of one of their beds. "I guess he must like coffee," one of the women said nervously to our guide. When asked if they were bothered by the sudden increase in activity by their poltergeist, one of the students said stoically, "Since they won't give us another room until next year, I guess we have to live with it."

The story continues.

Devon was in the process of taking Terry, one of our new guides, on a training tour. She was outside Stevens Hall and told the story. When she was finished, Terry said that she had been taking some classes at the college and spent a summer in the room just below the Blue Boy Room.

No one lived in the "Blue Boy Room" above her. She said that very often at 11:00 or 12:00 at night, she would hear the distinct sound of furniture being dragged across the floor just above her head. "That story answers my question," Terry said, "it's just him re-arranging the furniture in the room."

Not far from Stevens Hall, just past the chapel and across North Washington Street, is the infamous Pennsylvania Hall, once used as a bloody hospital during the battle. More than a century later it was the scene of not one, but several sightings of that same hospital scene complete with torn, wounded soldiers, recreated this time by their uneasy spirits.

One of Devon's friends works in Pennsylvania Hall. Just off her office is a small room that contains all the yearbooks produced by Gettysburg College from its inception to the present, containing the cumulative memories and images of former students, both living and long dead. There is an old wooden desk and chair in that room. As kind of a quaint display in the computer age, on the desk sits an old fashioned typewriter, complete with moving carriage for holding the paper.

Through the door to the seemingly benign static room, often her friend will hear the tap-tap-tap of the keys on the typewriter, or the chair pull out with a wooden scrape along the floor, or the sound of flipping pages of a book, as if someone were looking through one of the ancient yearbooks for a long-dead friend.

She said it used to scare her, but, like many of us, she became accustomed to the unseen others with whom we all share this life. She calls her ghosts the Typewriter Lady and the Page Turner Person and seems at ease with them, at least for now.

Pennsylvania Hall

Finally, Devon was giving a tour and discovered her group included an old friend. She had started the story of "The Party Ghost," about the young boy who seemed to appear in the older part of the house whenever renting college students would throw a party in the newer section. He was so real looking, patrons thought he was someone's younger brother visiting his Gettysburg College sibling. Try as they might, however, they could not induce him to join the party. It was as if he were stuck in the old Civil War section of the building…for all eternity.

A second story recounts a student studying in the basement hearing footsteps roaming the floor above his head, when all his housemates were gone. He followed their sound to the door to the basement and saw a light illuminate the other side of the door—but only as high up as a young person would stand. He opened the door and the light extinguished.

For reasons of privacy, our guides do not point out the actual building. Yet here was Devon's friend snapping picture after picture of that very building, as if she knew it was the source of the story.

After the tour Devon asked her friend if she knew the story of the house. Her associate told her that one of her daughter's friends and family had temporarily rented that house. Devon asked if her friends had anything strange happen in the house. "Oh, yeah," her friend said enthusiastically. Her own daughter would come home after a visit to the house and talk about the little boy that was always in the kitchen. Immediately Devon thought, "Party Ghost." Her friend recalled that her daughter said that the front door would open and close all the time, and no one came in or went out. She said she loved staying overnight there to see if the little boy would show up.

Realizing the rarity of a "visual"—an actual ghost sighting—Devon asked if they actually saw him. Her friend replied, "Yes. And that's why your story makes sense, that he would only light up the lower half of the door."

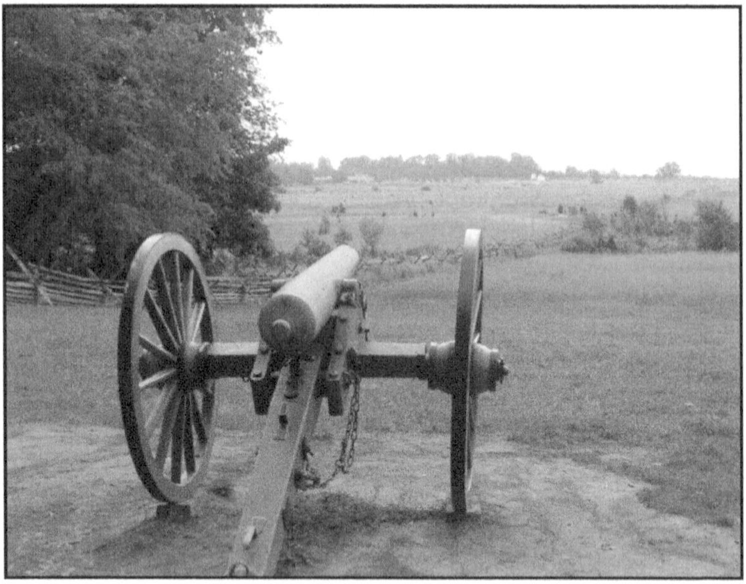

BEINGS OF LIGHT

The task is not to see what has never been seen before, but to think what has never been thought before about what you see every day.

—Erwin Schrödinger, Physicist

One of the most fascinating stories I collected about the Battle of Gettysburg was the story of a young man who was on the battlefield a few days after the battle. He was near the infamous Rose Farm, where so many human bodies were consigned to shallow unconsecrated graves without coffins, left to lie massed with former comrades presumably until the Great Day of Judgment.

It was nearing dark and he was passing a particularly large mound of earth which had recently been shoveled over scores of human remains, mutilated by shot and shell launched by their fellow humans within the last few days. As he passed, he saw to his amazement, a phosphorescent light hovering over this mound. He was convinced that it was the souls of the dead ascending to their Maker.

I suggested that what he saw would be explained by modern science as methane gas being released from the decomposing biological material beneath the ground.

After studying reports from all over the world, our frightened passer-by might have been closer to the real reason for the strange glow rising than we first gave him credit for.

Around the world, and throughout time, light anomalies have been witnessed by average individuals and the psychically gifted. They have been called "Will-o-the-Wisps," "Fairy Lights," "Earth lights," "Jack-o-lanterns," and "Spook Lights." Light anomalies have been associated with extra-terrestrials and their craft, which often glow or send a beam of light to interrupt human activities, sometimes by abducting the observers. Light, in the form of halos, appears in old paintings as an indication of divinity. In the very beginning, according to the Bible, God said, "Let there be light." "I am the light," Jesus said.

The *Ghosts of Gettysburg* series is filled with examples of light phenomena associated with the famous battle site.

Plum Run meanders through the fields below Little Round Top, traversing the valley formed by the smaller Round Top and Hauck's Ridge. Peaceful as it may seem to any visitor, the area was named, apparently by the soldiers or older guides who knew the soldiers who had fought through it, the Valley of Death. Tranquil, slow-moving Plum Run was re-christened, Bloody Run for the few hours in American History on July 2, 1863, when it ran red with the blood of human beings slain in the valley or the wounded able to crawl to it for water. It seems to particularly be an area prone to somehow replaying the scene that was enacted there on the night of July 2, after the slaughter had ceased. Numerous people have seen strange yellowish lights, like candles or candle lanterns, swaying through the valley, stopping, descending toward the ground as if being lowered to try and recognize a face contorted in death, or if the torn bloodied chest still moves, a sign that a soldier on the ground may have the glimmer of life yet in him.

Some of the older park rangers would mention how, on certain nights, particularly on the anniversary of the battle, what looked like campfires—hundreds—would flare up all along the sides of the South Mountain Range where, over a century before, they had flickered to cook coffee or warm some Confederate's last supper on earth before the gods of battle plucked him from this plane of existence.

And there was the ranger I worked with who, coming home from a conference, saw flickering campfires in the Wheatfield. It was too late to awaken her superior to go out and chase a few people camping illegally, but the next morning at daybreak she called him and they went out to roust the campers and perhaps even give them a hefty fine. But when they got to the site, there were no campers, no fires, no burned wood or scorched earth, not a remnant of a fire anywhere in the Wheatfield.

In general, and too numerous to mention individually, are the famous "orbs" that appear in photos of the town, out on the National Park and even indoors. There's recently been a trend on the Internet to label all photos of orbs as merely dust. While some, if not most, of the photos presented to me are dust too close to the lens and out-of-focus, or even more likely rain if it is precipitating when the photo was taken, "all"—like "never"—is far too encompassing a concept to be used when discussing orbs.

I have witnessed far too many orb light anomalies do strange things to rule them all as dust. I have seen them on videotape come out of walls and mirrors during EVP sessions, as if to touch my recorder to leave their voices; during playback I have watched them return, as if to listen to themselves again after untold years of silence. I have seen them on tape perform requests at the behest of paranormal researchers to move one way or another, or come back in front of the camera after they have seemingly left.

Then there was the large bright orb I saw in an infrared night vision scope that came *through* the roof of Sachs Covered Bridge, hover before my astonished eyes, do a ninety degree turn and shoot out through the latticework side of the bridge. And at the same bridge, once used by both armies for transport across Marsh Creek, I remember the video taken of several college students in March 1999, frightened by the noise of horses "charging" them, running towards the camera followed by seven or eight orbs, which "dodged" the stationary camera.

Not to mention the orb seen by my fellow paranormal investigator during a wrap up at East Cavalry Field that entered my van through the windshield, passed between us toward the back of the van, then was kind enough to stop there to have its image photographed.

In other words, some orbs seem to display a kind of intelligence in that they respond to living humans.

Also adding to the pool of knowledge about orbs is the fact that some individuals who are psychically gifted (like my fellow investigator at East Cavalry Field above) claim to actually see orbs with the naked eye. Those examples are not "dust too close to the lens."

As an experiment, I have attempted to photograph dust and have had little success in exactly replicating what I, or others, have captured that could be classified as typical orbs. So, the best conclusion I can come to as to what they are is that the jury is still out.

It seems that there is a connection between orbs, paranormal mist and localized temperature changes. My personal experience occurred on one of my first paranormal investigations with Pennsylvania ghost expert Rick Fisher. We were at the Point of Woods near the Virginia monument after dark. Using a thermal scanner he was picking up cold spots a short distance away. Some in the group were capturing photos of orbs where he pointed the scanner. Curious, I walked out to the spot where he directed me. Photos showed the orbs gathering closer to me. (For what reason, I still cannot comprehend. Were they attempting to collect energy from me, like when they steal it from batteries in electronic devices, or, showing an intelligence by just being curious?) Nevertheless, I felt an uncomfortable, increasing coldness until I removed myself from that area.

A letter I received seems to confirm my previous personal experience.

A man and some friends were investigating the famous Triangular Field one late October evening after dark. The Triangular Field, of course, is famous for the see-saw battle between Georgia and Texas Confederates and the 124th New York "Orange Blossoms" commanded by Col. Augustus van Horne Ellis, who insisted on riding his horse into the deadly fray because he wanted his men to know their officers were among them. It was suicide: he was killed when a bullet slammed into his brain via his forehead.

The investigators had the basic instrumentation to do a paranormal investigation: Thermal scanner and Electromagnetic Field (EMF) meter to detect anomalies, and a digital camera to record them. But, true to their history, the entities in the Triangular Field were exercising their energy thievery.

First, the "slave" flash attached to his camera died. He returned to his car to retrieve fresh batteries. The flash worked, but the camera, which he had just fully charged, showed a low battery warning. He discovered that the camera was giving a false indication, since he could continue to take photos throughout the evening.

As they walked through the gate and into the field, he could see in his screen viewfinder orbs coming from the wood line edging the field and heading towards him. But they bypassed him and went to his friends carrying the other equipment. He began taking shots of his friends and every one showed the orbs actually gathering around them. Just as he was about to mention that fact to them, one of his friends shouted that the temperature according to the thermal scanner had dropped from 33 degrees to minus two degrees! The person holding the scanner called out that she could feel it and that she was extremely cold. Her fellow investigator with the EMF meter moved towards her and reported that she, too, felt the cold.

The male investigator watched through his viewfinder as orbs congregated around the two women in a vortex, "like an 'orb blizzard'" he wrote, until they began to dissipate. As the orbs faded, a strange mist began to rise up behind them—they all saw it and he caught it with his camera. The mist rose, spiraled, and moved down the slope of the Triangular Field.

Returning home and downloading the pictures to his computer, the moving mist particularly caught his attention.

His friend who was in the picture happened to be behind him as the photo appeared on the screen and voiced what was going through his head: "Don't tell me that's a horse and rider behind us!"

Because the human brain has evolved to recognize shapes in matrixes, it can be fooled into seeing things that aren't necessarily in existence. But the fact that his fellow researcher saw the figure before he had the opportunity to say anything is as close to an independent affirmation as we can hope to get. Was it Col. Ellis, rising up and riding down the hill to enter the fight once again so long after his death? We can never know.

But "orbs" are not the only light anomaly associated with the supernatural.

There are the numerous sightings around Gettysburg of a "woman in white". In fact, so many, that the sightings may have to be known by the plural, "women" in white.

Besides the original sightings in the Spangler's Spring area—which must have been enough in number to start the legend—there was the sighting by a man when he was a teenager as he passed through the area on his bicycle one evening. Then there were the two nurses who, while parked in the lot, actually saw her materialize among the rocks near them. There was the couple that lived just a few hundred yards from Spangler's Spring who saw her repeatedly floating along their upstairs hallway, who a famed psychic identified as a nun.

I received a letter from a woman in Wisconsin who had visited Gettysburg with her husband and two friends. They were in the parking lot of Devil's Den just after dark. Devil's Den, with its diabolic name, monstrous boulders, and terrifying history of struggle and death, is ominous enough in broad daylight; at night it can evoke sheer terror in even the most solid individuals. They decided to leave.

As they wound their way out of the natural labyrinth she glanced up and saw "a lady in a long dress glowing white." She described the dress as a long "gown" of the 1800s period. The glowing woman stood near the top of the Den by some trees. The woman in the car yelled for the driver to stop and inquired if anyone could see her. She continued to watch for about five seconds, when the woman in white "vaporized." While the apparition was very close to the roadway and she got a good enough look at her to describe what she wore, none of her friends apparently saw her.

Devil's Den

There are the scores of sightings of glowing spectral human-like forms scattered throughout the *Ghosts of Gettysburg* books: My own sighting behind my house on Carlisle Street of the mist that morphed from a low blob on the ground into an upright moving column with a bluish core; there was the woman down the street from me who stayed up late typing papers and was taunted by a bluish column until it formed into the full body of an 18th Century highwayman; and there are the blue columns of light that appear periodically on East Cemetery Hill—at least three times—to our amazed *Ghosts of Gettysburg Candlelight Walking Tours* customers, and even more amazed guides.

Bluish light seem to appear as one of the predominant hues when there is color involved.

In *Ghosts of Gettysburg IV* I wrote about a group of college students who had tempted fate by using a Ouija Board at Devil's Den. It spelled out "Airck," which they interpreted as a man named "Eric" and "QD" which they thought indicated a woman: "Cutie." Before they closed the board, one of them asked the entities to meet them at their car in the parking lot. Freaked out, the rest began to scamper toward the car. From the woods across Bloody Run they saw a bluish light emerge, then form into a couple strolling toward their car. The students got in a race to see who would reach the car first…and won. But as they sped away, the driver saw in the rear-view mirror the bluish-tinged forms of two people in Civil War era garb watching them leave.

Woods across from Bloody Run

But a photograph taken of the Triangular Field near Devil's Den hanging in the *Ghosts of Gettysburg* Headquarters building shows a human-like form, seemingly bent forward like an advancing soldier; the light-form is multicolored, like a rainbow.

White is perhaps the most prevalent color, however. In a Civil War era farmhouse I investigated for *Ghosts of Gettysburg III*, the owner once followed a ball of light down his hallway; in Stevens Hall on the college campus, a white light shot across the room. In a redux of the famous "Party Ghost" story of a young man who shows himself during college parties, but seemingly stuck in the older section of the house, cannot participate; after hearing footsteps, a student saw a light beaming from under a door until he opened it and found himself cast into darkness. Finally there was the night clerk who, upon inspecting a light burning in the basement of the James Gettys Hotel, found the light came from the figure of a Confederate soldier, who backed into the wall and plunged the clerk into night-like gloom.

In *Ghosts of Gettysburg IV* there was the photo of a gold crucifix that appeared above the famous Point of Woods in the Confederate lines, already purported to be haunted. And in the *Ghosts of Gettysburg* tour headquarters, our manager observed a ball of light float into the office and explode with a loud "pop" just above her head.

And from the sixth book in the series, in a modern hotel located on the battlefield, there is the witnessing of a white glowing disembodied arm that emerges from the darkness to disturb a comfortable night's sleep by a heavy push—twice—then recedes back into the darkness whence it came. Then, in the same hotel, there was the floating female limb, hovering in the air to disturb an innocent visitor's sleep.

From *Ghosts of Gettysburg VII*, there is the testimony of the manager of the Gettysburg and Northern Railroad who was in the infamous (and very haunted) engine house where he saw a glowing, "misty, translucent form" between the engines that mocked his approach by backing away, and teased his inquisitiveness by approaching him again when he backed off. It finally ended its game, removing itself from the scene by leaving through the solid wall.

So these phosphorescent phenomena appear seemingly at will throughout the supernatural history of Gettysburg up to the present day. But is there some connection with the light anomalies to the thousands of soldiers who had their lives snuffed out in the streets and environs of America's most famous small town?

It just so happens that scientists have determined that from conception until death—and a bit after that—humans are "beings of light." We exude throughout our existence electromagnetism in the form of photons or light particles and waves.

We know that visible light exists in varying frequencies within the electromagnetic spectrum. Some paranormal theorists believe that ghosts can become visible when they lower or raise their vibrational frequency to the visible spectrum or when they are surrounded by mist or smoke that allows reflection of the visible light, just like a beam of a flashlight can only be seen when there is fog or smoke. The question is: is there a *conscious intention* behind this change in frequency, indicating a surviving personality regulating it? A personality as in a once living *person*?

Perhaps this is why at Gettysburg and other battlefields, paranormal investigators' electronic equipment is affected, both positively—by indicating the presence of electromagnetic fields and recording unheard and unseen voices and images—and negatively—by batteries dying and equipment failures.

Perhaps the long-dead soldiers are not so far away after all.

SOURCES

Coco, Gregory A., *Killed in Action: Eyewitness Accounts of the Last Moments of 100 Union Soldiers Who Died at Gettysburg.* Gettysburg: Thomas Publications, 1992.

Ibid. *A Strange and Blighted Land, Gettysburg: The Aftermath of a Battle.* Gettysburg: Thomas Publications, 1995.

Jung, C. G. *Jung on Synchronicity and the Paranormal*, Roderick Main, Ed. Princeton: Princeton University Press, 1998.

Nesbitt, Mark. *Ghosts of Gettysburg: Spirits, Apparitions and Haunted Places of the Battlefield.* Seven Volumes. Gettysburg: Second Chance Publications, 1991-2011.

Opie, John M., *A Rebel Cavalryman with Lee Stuart and Jackson.* Chicago, W. B. Conkey Company, 1899. Reprint, Morningside Bookshop, Dayton, Ohio, 1972.

Pfanz, Harry W. *Gettysburg: The First Day.* Chapel Hill and London: The University of North Carolina Press, 2001.

Pfanz, Harry W. *Gettysburg: The Second Day.* Chapel Hill and London: The University of North Carolina Press, 1987.

Stewart, George R. *Pickett's Charge: A Microhistory of the Final Attack at Gettysburg, July 3, 1863.* Boston: Houghton Mifflin Company, 1959.

Viola, Herman J., ed., *The Memoirs of Charles Henry Veil: A Soldier's Recollections of the Civil War and the Arizona Territory.* New York: Orion Books, 1993.

gettysburgdaily.com/bennings-brigade-battle-walk, by Ranger Raffi Andonian, accessed, November 8, 2017, 5:32 P.M.

civilwar.org/learn/articles/battle-fairfield, accessed 10/26/17, 11:43 A.M.

"We Are Made of Light: Scientific Evidence," from http://humansarefree.com/2014/04/we-are-made-of-light-scientific-evidence.html.

ACKNOWLEDGMENTS

Many thanks go out to the following people for their contributions to this work:

Jill Brandt, Corrine Brownholtz, Chet Crist, Mary Duval, Kristina M. Fay, Ann Griffith, Maggie Glenn, John Green, David L. Hallett, Adam Halpin and Nicole Booth, Joe Howard, Dale Kaczmarek, Shannon Keeler, Nicole, and their housemates, Sandy Kime, Nicole Lenart, Christine Lewin, Mike Payden, Julie Pellegrino, Jan Portwood, Jeff Prechtel, Kathryn L. Preston, Katherine Ramsland, W. J. Romeo, Ph.D., Brian K. Senft and Dr. Charles Emmons, Barbara Simon, Krista Smith, Dan Todd of D&S Paranormal Investigators in New Jersey, and Clair and Linda Zeiders.

But most of all, I thank my editor, inspiration, muse, reason for everything, and luckily, my wife, Carol who turns my words into books and my world into bliss.

ABOUT THE AUTHOR

I started my career in Gettysburg as a National Park Service Ranger/Historian back in the 1970s. I knew that I wanted to be a writer, so after five years with the NPS, I got the crazy idea that I should start my own research and writing company. I became fascinated by, and started collecting, the ghost stories of the Gettysburg area. My first *Ghosts of Gettysburg* book came out in 1991. Since then, I have written over twenty books covering topics of historical interest, as well as the paranormal. My stories have been seen on *The History Channel, A&E, The Discovery Channel, The Travel Channel, Unsolved Mysteries, The Biography Channel*, and numerous regional television shows and heard on *Coast to Coast AM*, and regional radio.

In 1994, I started the commercially successful *Ghosts of Gettysburg Candlelight Walking Tours*.

Other books in print and/or ebooks by Mark Nesbitt:
Ghosts of Gettysburg
Ghosts of Gettysburg II
Ghosts of Gettysburg III
Ghosts of Gettysburg IV

Ghosts of Gettysburg V
Ghosts of Gettysburg VI
Ghosts of Gettysburg VII

Civil War Ghost Trails
A Ghost Hunters Field Guide: Gettysburg & Beyond
Fredericksburg & Chancellorsville: A Ghost Hunters Field Guide
Haunted Pennsylvania
The Big Book of Pennsylvania Ghost Stories

Cursed in Pennsylvania
Cursed in Virginia

Blood & Ghosts: Haunted Crime Scene Investigations
Haunted Crime Scenes

If The South Won Gettysburg
35 Days to Gettysburg: The Campaign Diaries of Two American Enemies (Reprinted as The Gettysburg Diaries: War Journals of Two American Adversaries)
Rebel Rivers: A Guide to Civil War Sites on the Potomac, Rappahannock, York, and James
Saber and Scapegoat: J.E.B. Stuart and the Gettysburg Controversy
Through Blood and Fire: The Selected Civil War Papers of Major General Joshua Chamberlain

Connect with **Mark Nesbitt** on Social Media:
facebook.com/mark.v.nesbitt
twitter.com/hauntgburg
markvnesbitt.wordpress.com
instagram.com/hauntgburg
linkedin.com/in/scpublications
goodreads.com/author/show/19835.Mark_Nesbitt

Made in the USA
Columbia, SC
12 November 2018